Praise for **The Mirrored Door**

"Ellen Connelly Taaffe's image of the 'mirrored door' brilliantly and accurately describes women's tendency to second-guess themselves when they bump up against barriers at work. Gazing into that mirror and asking, 'Is it me?' can paralyze us and make it difficult to take action. Ellen's work is a powerful corrective to the endless focus on 'imposter syndrome,' which pathologizes self-doubt rather than offering a path forward. In this wise and humane book, she shows how women can address the internal barriers most likely to hold them back. Highly recommended!"

SALLY HELGESEN, bestselling author of *How Women Rise, Rising Together,* and *The Female Advantage*

"*The Mirrored Door* is an inspiring guide for women looking to advance in their careers. Ellen Connelly Taaffe outlines the external and internal biases that lead to women getting stuck in their jobs. Through engaging stories, she offers frameworks and advice on how to move past these obstacles and create the future we all want."

DEEPA PURUSHOTHAMAN, author of *The First, the Few, the Only*

"*The Mirrored Door* is a must-read for career-minded women who aspire to more. Ellen Connelly Taaffe connects insightful research, shares engaging stories, and thoughtfully reveals what might have once worked but could now be in the way. This book informs and inspires women to take charge of their careers."

DORIE CLARK, *Wall Street Journal*-bestselling author of *The Long Game*

"*The Mirrored Door* is the book that every female leader—of all ages and stages—needs to read. If you have ever struggled in your career, this book will provide you with valuable insights to identify and overcome the challenges that are preventing you from achieving the success that you want. Ellen Connelly Taaffe is a kind, wise mentor who provides you with the road map you need to create the future you want. I wish I had this book when I started my career."

TRICIA MONTALVO TIMM, board director, former general counsel at Looker, and author of *Embrace the Power of You*

"*The Mirrored Door* is a terrific primer for career-oriented women to create their own successful path, navigating through the systemic biases that women face in today's workplace. It's a compelling blueprint by former business executive and current professor, Ellen Connelly Taaffe."

CARTER CAST, clinical professor of entrepreneurship at the Kellogg School of Management and author of *The Right— and Wrong—Stuff*

"Be the protagonista! That's what practitioner-turned-professor Ellen Connelly Taaffe teaches women (and any leader who wants to sponsor women) how to do with her splendid storytelling and actionable advice. Ellen describes herself as the 'professor full of doubt,' but there's no doubt about this book: if you want to shatter the glass ceiling, you'll open *The Mirrored Door*. This book belongs alongside Sally Helgesen's *How Women Rise*— welcome to the canon of literature sure to inspire the next generation of women leaders."

WHITNEY JOHNSON, CEO of Disruption Advisors and *Wall Street Journal*-bestselling author of *Smart Growth*

"Ellen Connelly Taaffe cleverly focuses on the one thing any woman can do to power her career: burst through the self-created 'mirrored door' that often holds us back. This book is a compelling manual for banishing self-doubt and grabbing your desired and deserved future!"

GENA COX, PhD, executive coach, speaker, and author of *Leading Inclusion*

"Ellen Connelly Taaffe brings a depth of knowledge and breadth of personal experience to every page. All women, regardless of career stage, will see themselves more clearly and be better equipped to step through the 'mirrored door' after reading this book."

LAURIE WEINGART, coauthor of *The No Club*

"While women often say they experience self-doubt and imposter syndrome, Ellen Connelly Taaffe's excellent book points out that the system—through ingrained biases and outdated work practices—is designed to make us feel that way. She offers ways that each of us can pivot our thinking away from self-blame, and, through a series of journal prompts, gives readers a chance to reflect on how they can have a healthier relationship to work and achievement."

SARAH KAPLAN, director of the Institute for Gender and the Economy (GATE) at the University of Toronto's Rotman School of Management

"This incisive, inviting guidebook surveys the challenges high-achieving women face in the workplace and shares fresh advice for navigating obstacles both inner and outer."

PUBLISHERS WEEKLY

"*The Mirrored Door* opens up the conversation for all women who are seeking to grow professionally and personally, no matter their stage in life. Ellen Connelly Taaffe generously shares her life and professional experiences while weaving in research-based evidence and the stories of women who navigated male-dominated corporate cultures while discovering their own gender biases that are so deeply ingrained in each of us. This book is an enlightening and practical guide for all women who seek to leverage their talents and power—and make a difference wherever they land."

TAMMY GOOLER LOEB, award-winning author of *Work from the Inside Out*

"*The Mirrored Door* is like having a caring, wise mentor show you the ropes of how to navigate the workplace and take charge of your own career and life. I wish it had been around for me to read at several different points in my career."

ANNE LESTER, former managing director of JPMorgan Asset Management, board director, speaker, and author of *Your Best Financial Life*

"If you lead women or are a woman, you must read *The Mirrored Door*. Ellen Connelly Taaffe has brilliantly written an inspiring, yet practical leadership book that is sure to become a go-to guide for aspiring and experienced career women and their allies. Through storytelling, research, and personal experience, she reveals what holds women back and what we can do about it. I wish I had it earlier in my career. Highly recommend!"

LISA LUTOFF-PERLO, vice chair of external affairs at Royal Caribbean Group, former CEO of Celebrity Cruises, board director, and author of *Making Waves*

ELLEN CONNELLY TAAFFE

KELLOGG SCHOOL OF MANAGEMENT

THE MIRRORED DOOR

Break Through the
Hidden Barrier That Locks
Successful Women in Place

Cataloguing in publication information is
available from Library and Archives Canada.
ISBN 978-1-77458-329-6 (paperback)
ISBN 978-1-77458-330-2 (ebook)

Page Two
pagetwo.com

Edited by Kendra Ward
Copyedited by Steph VanderMeulen
Proofread by Alison Strobel
Cover and interior design by Fiona Lee
Printed and bound in Canada by Friesens
Distributed in Canada by Raincoast Books
Distributed in the US and internationally by Macmillan

23 24 25 26 27   5 4 3 2 1

ellentaaffe.com

To my daughters, Maggie and Katie.

*Thank you for giving me the greatest role
I've ever had and for teaching and inspiring
me every day. May you have the courage to
break through the mirrored door and leave
it wide open so others may find their way.*

THE
MIRRORED
DOOR

Contents

A Note about This Work

THE STORIES IN this book speak to issues and situations women face in their professional lives. In many cases, I have created pseudonyms and altered specific details of their careers and lives. In some examples, I've created a composite based on similar narratives from multiple women. Any resemblance to any real person with similar names and/or personal details and/or employment characteristics is purely coincidental.

I am not a researcher; I am a dot connector. Where possible, I've attempted to connect the many facets of women's career experiences to research findings. While there is a growing body of evidence-based insights regarding gender in the workplace, there are gaps, and many observations are drawn from studies done without regard to intersectionality or gender fluidity. Much of the research is United States based. Clearly, women are not a monolith. That said, the research we do have can help us understand our starting point. I'm hopeful that in the years to come more will be studied and understood regarding marginalized genders, race, color, sexual orientation, ability, nationality, education and income levels, neurodiversity, and others.

The views expressed in this book are my own.

Introduction
In Front of the Mirrored Door

"**Y**OU'RE THAT professor who's full of doubt, right?"

This was not my finest moment as a faculty member, or the smartest way for my student to greet me on the first day of class. Still, I tried to take it in stride.

"Yes, I do have my doubts," I said. "I've learned that many, if not most, people do too. We simply don't talk about it. This is especially true when we've had some success and are striving for something more, like the next level of leadership. We come up against bias and other obstacles, and it's disorienting. It can lead to doubt." I noticed the thirtysomething woman's eyes welling up. "It's more common than you'd think," I added.

After a pause, she straightened her shoulders and looked squarely at me. "That's why I took your class and arrived early. I hope you can help."

"That's why I am here," I said, smiling.

This young woman and I talked for a while longer that day about the challenges high-achieving women face in the workplace. I could tell she had not heard such candor from a successful woman before, and that perhaps conversations with

3

her peers were less than forthcoming. I had sensed the same when I told other students, workshop participants, and audience members at talks I give about times I received difficult feedback, was passed over for a promotion and continually underestimated, and when I finally set boundaries after a lifetime of nonstop yeses—all experiences that tested my confidence, to say the least.

Prior to that quarter, I had shared my doubts publicly in an article called "3 Tips for Conquering Self-Doubt at Work," published in *Kellogg Insight*, an online magazine that features the research and opinions of faculty at the Kellogg School of Management at Northwestern University. When I joined the school in 2016, I built the Women's Leadership Program for MBA women, and I continue to oversee it, teach the Personal Leadership Insights course, and coach Executive Education participants. Now, it seemed I had developed a reputation.

The article had resonated, reaching more than thirty-one thousand views in the first few months, and was picked up by *Business Insider*, *Entrepreneur*, multiple trade organizations, and LinkedIn as the Editor's Pick of the Week in August 2021. I started getting LinkedIn notes from lots of people I didn't know, including high-ranking executives, telling me they feel these doubts almost daily. I was shocked that people with amazing profiles, from emerging leaders to mid-career management to CEOs, experienced these feelings.

About a month later, a fellow board director shared the article with everyone on our organization's board. Although I had previously been thrilled about the article's reach and appeal, I suddenly felt exposed. People who knew me were now learning my personal stories of the self-doubt I had been confronting, in one form or another, since early in my career. At the next meeting, I entered the room feeling a bit embarrassed that I was found out.

But much to my surprise, the board had deeper, more vulnerable conversations than ever before in the days that followed. My male peers told me they were initially surprised I had doubts, but now they were hearing the same truths from female colleagues, wives, and daughters. The article had opened conversations in their households and during their business meetings. I had assumed my fellow board members would think I was the weak link, but the opposite was true. All this reinforced a growing conviction in me: for women to genuinely gain more seats at the table, we must collectively recognize the internal and external biases that can block us and distort our self-view. My big reveal showed me that my voice matters, as do the voices of all women.

A Hidden Barrier

Women don't always feel safe enough to be vulnerable and ask for the guidance they need, especially in a glamorized world of girl-boss profiles and curated social media posts. Too many smart women carry the belief that problems in their careers "lie within." We were told we could do anything with our education, hard work, and ambition, and yet no one told us the vital message that our careers will be difficult. Inevitably, as we advance, we face challenges. We double down on what worked in the past but find those strategies no longer achieve the outcomes we want, and we feel like we did something wrong. Sometimes our plan to work harder is a less-than-healthy way to cover up fear and doubt. We often don't ask for the help we desperately need so as not to show others we don't have all the answers. We see issues with the workplace but still wonder what went wrong and why we are suddenly stuck. A new company might offer a change, but our suspicions lurk under

Too many smart women carry the belief that problems in their careers "lie within."

the surface: *maybe it's me*. We churn inside and hesitate to risk new actions.

For most women, navigating workplaces that were built for a different time and different employee population is a challenge. With women completing college and graduate programs and entering the workplace in greater numbers and with higher aspirations than ever before, I thought we would be on our way to breaking the glass ceiling. But becoming a leader when you haven't seen someone who looks like you lead is not easy.

Women are still held to a prevailing male leadership model and the resulting perceptions and institutional obstacles. But another dynamic is also at play, and it too may lock us in place. I call it the "mirrored door." We encounter it when we reflect inward and question our readiness for and worthiness of an opportunity. Instead of going for it, we assess that we cannot. When this self-judgment leads to hesitation, we stop growing or get left behind, despite our hard work and comparable performance. This hidden barrier blocks our path when we otherwise could move forward despite uncertainty. Our male counterparts more frequently jump at chances with far more ease, while we wait and expend time and energy to feel more prepared, certain, and confident.

When we second-guess ourselves at the mirrored door, we rob ourselves of valuable learning from trial and error, and of confidence earned from taking smart risks and recovering after a stumble. To be sure, we are locked out at times. But the metaphor of the mirrored door suggests that, confronted with our own self-image, we may also be locking ourselves in.

At Kellogg, I learned that today's women are prepared to work and lead yet face the same hurdles I did years ago. I dove into the workplace research and was dismayed to see how little things had changed. When some women escaped the corporate world to attend business school, I heard the surprise and disappointment about their early work experiences. I saw that society seemed to have glossed over the challenges we face, navigating workplaces full of old systems, bias, and a lack of role models, amid a greedy culture that rewards careers at the height of women's childbearing and caregiving years.

From my teaching, coaching, and investigation into existing research, I learned about others' lived experiences and the higher hurdles faced at the intersection of gender with color, ethnicity, nationality, sexual orientation, ability, income, and other factors. Though many if not most studies reference white cisgender women, I believe that the mirrored door applies across marginalized genders and populations, especially given the sense that one's marginalization can lead to working twice as hard to be seen as just as good. I've also heard from men sharing that they face a mirrored door of their own. While I believe that to be true, given our "man up" culture, this book highlights what women uniquely and more frequently face. My hope is that men will read this book with the intent to become real allies for the girls and women in their lives and to change the systems that propagate the mirrored door. If it helps them consider the expectations and doubts they may face, that's a bonus.

Unlocking the Future We Desire

My goal with *The Mirrored Door* is to share the realities I see and to enlighten women on their way. Knowledge is power, and when we can learn the lessons from the past and the challenges of the present, we can choose a new future for ourselves.

This is not a quick-fix book. It is a guidebook for what you might face and how you might stretch yourself to meet the moment and go after what you want on your terms. Part One is a deep dive into how and why we formed habits that work for and against us. Part Two explores the five perils of success (preparing to perfection, eagerly pleasing, fitting the mold, working pedal to the metal, performing patiently) and how we might uncover and mitigate the blind spots. Part Three reveals the gifts we earn on the other side of the mirrored door when we connect more deeply to ourselves, each other, and our future. Through reading this book, you will start to unravel what you have learned about being a successful woman, uncover how well-intentioned messages might be in your way, and open up a new mindset—a way of being on your own terms.

I encourage you to take in *The Mirrored Door* with a journal at your side, friends to discuss it with, a lens of curiosity and self-reflection, and compassion for yourself and others. When you can unravel the past and understand how culture has conditioned our beliefs and influences our workplace systems, you have more freedom to choose what you bring with you to your company and your future. It will take some letting go and building up, along with experimentation and practice. You are no stranger to hard work. You can do this. And when you do, you will step into the lead role of your career and life in a new, rewarding way. You will empower yourself every time you greet opportunity and unlock, open, and pass over the threshold of the mirrored door, leaving the door ajar for those who follow.

PART ONE

BREAK OPEN: HOW WE SEE OURSELVES

In Part One, we will dive into the well-intentioned norms that we learn as we grow up and how these messages are reinforced in school, family, friendships, and our society. We'll unravel how this socialization prepares women to succeed academically and initially in our careers but may also carry self-judgment and hesitation later. We'll explore how our ingrained yet unreasonably high expectations combine with workplace cultures that are stuck in the past, and how biases contribute to our unrealistic reflections, which can unfairly distort our self-perception, seed doubt, and hold us back.

Raise Your Hand, Raise Your Future

. . . .

*"My coach said I run like a girl. And I said
if he ran a little faster, he could too."*
MIA HAMM

ICHELLE WAS the golden girl. When she was selected to succeed her boss, she was thrilled with getting the nod and the mentorship that came with being groomed for the job. For years, she had aspired to become a chief marketing officer and invested a lot of time and effort to make it happen, including taking several challenging roles that made her stronger. She worked long hours in the office, traveled extensively, and dedicated time at night and on weekends to keep up with it all. She was often tapped for extra commitments and welcomed each new volunteer opportunity. She was energized by this very full work life and countered her intense career with the purchase of a new home that would become a respite. She felt as though she had it all.

After two years of close interaction with senior leaders to prepare her, she began to sense a change in her boss's attitude toward her. No matter how hard she tried, she could not shake the feeling that something had shifted. She began to add up vague signs that made her fear the assumed promotion wasn't a done deal. And the signals grew louder.

A peer began to attend several of her department meetings without a clear role beyond her boss saying, "I think it is a good idea." Michelle struggled to get on her busy boss's calendar. Though he had taken on more responsibilities, she began to feel shut out. Then, she got feedback from him to elevate her executive presence, which she had previously thought was one of her strengths.

Michelle's rising anxieties fueled an extensive amount of planning, hard work, and stress before every meeting. She spent hours preparing for the limited encounters with her boss and led elaborate pre-meetings with her team to increase the odds of a successful meeting with no surprises. These gave her a sense of certainty and readiness.

Her team practiced multiple times ahead of the annual strategic planning session, assuring her she would nail this presentation. As the meeting began, though, she became unnerved. Not even on the attendee list, her peer waltzed in, sat next to her boss, and whispered to him throughout Michelle's presentation. All seemed to go as planned until her peer lobbed several unanticipated questions and skeptical comments about the most innovative part of her plan. Just when she thought her boss would shut down her coworker, he instead amplified the concerns, complimented the peer's insightful inquiry, and asked Michelle for follow-up work before he would commit. Michelle felt tongue-tied when responding and summarizing next steps.

When her boss ruled against her recommendation and sided with her peer, she felt bruised and battle weary. She wondered to herself why she didn't speak up and show the extensive analysis that supported her recommendations. Worse yet, during a break, her boss seemed charmed by her peer. Her stomach dropped. She began to suspect that maybe she was the heir "apparently not."

During one of her many late nights at the office, Michelle accidentally saw a succession plan on the printer and two names on the backfill list for her boss. At first, she comforted herself with the thought that HR required at least two names. She told herself that was simply good planning for the leadership team. As she continued to get scant face time with and feedback from her boss, she feared her future role had slipped through her hands. She no longer felt like the golden girl and doubted her every move.

I met Michelle when she was in the throes of this situation, racking her brain about what had happened to her status and track to promotion. Her workload and everything she was doing to prove herself sounded truly staggering.

I'd been there, and you've probably been there too. You may be there right now. We think we are doing everything right, following all the rules, but somehow, we end up overlooked, undervalued, and/or overworked. Is it the glass ceiling? Is it the boss or the company culture? What if there is something more? What if this problem begins earlier than in the workplace?

Perfection Is Not the Price of Admission

Several years ago, I got a much-needed lesson while sitting in on the first day of student orientation as a new business school professor. I sat in awe of these amazing, bright, and shiny twenty-something students from around the globe. With so much possibility in the air, there was a thrilling sense that this was the start of something big.

The students smiled, wide-eyed as they listened intently to the keynote speaker, hanging on every story. When she finished, she said, "Tell me what's on your minds."

Dozens of hands shot up. One man asked her about her boldest career move, another questioned the timing and risk of her company changes, and a third asked for her biggest regret. I was pleased to hear so many intriguing questions and her insightful answers.

My grin disappeared when I noticed a pattern. I counted the questions and saw that every single one came from men in the class. I waited and waited for this to change, but it did not. The women never raised their hands.

When I shared my observation with Melanie, the administrator that had booked our speaker, she said, "Yeah, that usually happens. Sometimes in the classroom too."

My heart sank. I thought back to when I was twenty-two years old and had circled my dream school in a book called *The Insider's Guide to the Top Ten Business Schools*. No one knew I had bought the book. No one knew about my dream. Going to business school was always a few years out. I would look at that circled school in the book every so often and think, *Not yet*.

I contemplated applying to business school for a decade. Even though I had solid work experience in my twenties, I always found a way to tell myself, *You're not ready*. Each year, I racked up a list of reasons it was not the right time or I would never get in: *I don't have enough experience. I went to a state school. I'm a first-generation college student. There are no MBAs in my family. I do not test well. I can't afford it. How will I compete with all the other students?*

Now in my thirties, I finally declared my MBA wish out loud to my husband, Ned. After talking through what this would mean so early in our marriage, I took the chance and applied. More than twenty-five years later, I still remember announcing the good news, with acceptance letter in hand, to my extended family at a backyard barbecue.

At my own orientation, I was proud to be realizing this dream and felt filled with potential. Yet sadly, my pride and anticipation were over-matched by a sudden sense that every hand I shook that day belonged to someone with much more experience and gravitas than I had. When I surveyed the big auditorium and counted on two hands the number of women classmates in a sea of men, I confirmed my lack of belonging and imagined an admissions error. I was at the threshold of my goal and found myself flat-footed with doubt.

Two decades later, after my corporate career, I rejoined my dream school and alma mater, the Kellogg School of Management at Northwestern University, as a clinical faculty member in the management and organizations department. I was thrilled to design and run the Women's Leadership Program. I believed that the statistics of more millennial women than men graduating from college, and the increasing number of top MBA programs including 40-plus percent women, would eventually lead to a major crack in the glass ceiling. After all, I had signed on to a mission to advance women to the C-suite to break through the invisible barrier that limits women from ascending to the uppermost levels. I felt called to do this work. In an inspired moment, I even changed my LinkedIn profile summary to include my mission: "More seats at the table."

But I learned quickly that gaining more seats was simply not enough. Here I was at this orientation, new in my job, surprised and frustrated with the women I would soon be teaching, mostly because I saw myself in them. I had expected that their generation would have let go of perfection and the accompanying hesitation. I had thought, given their education, accomplishments, and readiness, they might dominate the discussions. I viewed millennials as the generation that would take risks and change the world. After all, they didn't have the burden of being pioneers or one of the few women at the table. Why didn't they understand that so many had cleared the path before them so that their voices would be heard?

I knew from the school's acceptance criteria that the women we admitted were off-the-charts smart and had made the most of their twenties. The lack of participation I had witnessed didn't add up, and I wanted to learn more. Perhaps it was a sign of something else.

At the orientation break, I rushed to the coffee stands to see for myself. There I met several women and found them engaging, brilliant, and accomplished, maybe more so than the men. One had started her own tech company and sold two rounds of financing. Another woman, who taught for Teach for America, had turned around the literacy rates of her students. A third woman was already a manager in a top-tier consulting firm with a growing expertise in health-care marketing. These women clearly "leaned in" and were successful. Why didn't they realize they brought so much of that value to their MBA program? By staying silent until they constructed the perfect question, they held themselves back, just as I had. And the crowd also missed hearing their unique perspectives.

During my own MBA years, I eventually worked through my self-doubt. Simply put, taking more risks in the face of fear at that transition changed my life, for the first time as a student and then the second time as a clinical professor. I have climbed the corporate ladder, become a board director, and now teach leadership. Yet, I seriously wonder: What if I'd never taken that leap and applied for the MBA? And what took me so long?

To be sure, there may be areas to develop and prepare for the next step, but many times, we women underestimate our qualifications and realistic readiness. If my students, with so much more opportunity than I had, did not feel ready to raise their hands, perhaps these issues were less generational and more gender induced. I realize now that when we hold back, it costs us—our influence, our upward mobility, our peace of mind. Our silence is not only deafening; it is defeating.

The Long-Term Trade-Off

I began to wonder about my own workplace experiences and that of the executive women I coach outside of Kellogg. I thought about when we felt something was amiss or we were stuck. I recalled so many ambitious women who performed well, were seen in a positive light, didn't make mistakes, yet faced their own hesitancy well into a successful career. The common threads between us all seemed to be a pattern of massive preparation; years of hard work; playing the part to please others; and safe, face-saving choices in meetings, one-on-one interactions, and career moves. We assumed the identity of a person who always has the right answer and approach, takes care of everyone else, and keeps the peace.

We think of ourselves as the A student, the dependable one, the good girl, the adult in the room who is conscientious and likeable and who doesn't rock the boat. We are achievers. We are pleasant. We are the glue that holds teams, households, and friends together. We care what others think—a lot. Maybe too much. We take all these wonderful traits into the workplace, where they are badly needed. This approach works for a while as we build reputations as people who can absolutely be counted on to execute and deliver. But for so many women, something happens on the way to middle management and the C-suite.

In countless coaching sessions, I have heard women share with me that while seemingly doing everything that was outlined for them, they felt flat-footed, stuck in self-judgment, surprised by new feedback, or abruptly derailed by a workplace designed for a different time *and* by their own mindsets. Suddenly, their approach, which had previously been rewarded, was undermined either by bosses looking for more "gravitas" or executive presence, or by their own doubts. They weren't prepared for the dynamics of the corporate ladder and the expectation that they take smart risks, share opinions, and convey a strong presence that seemed to come naturally for men. Their ambition to lead others, make a meaningful impact, and influence the direction had not shifted, but their foundation felt shaky.

We are taught early that playing the part and awaiting permission is the way it works. Our instinctive approach to perfect, please, and prepare enables women to excel early, but it gets in the way of what we want and what could be next.

The Mirrored Door

My contention is that we women face a powerful barrier, an often invisible obstacle that we must break through to make it anywhere close to bigger leadership roles. It is not the glass ceiling—it is the mirrored door. The mirrored door is what makes us reflect inward and question our readiness. The mirrored door is our own self-criticism and doubt that stand between us and the future we desire. It obstructs our view of what's beyond us and tricks us into believing our limiting self-perceptions. This leads to overthinking and, frequently, under-acting. We question our skills, fit, ideas, and others' judgment, and we slow or halt our momentum. We hesitate, avoid risk, and forget the value we can bring.

We hold ourselves back preparing, perfecting, pleasing, portraying, pushing ourselves, and even policing our words and actions, as if we cannot pass over the threshold until we see certainty and perfection in that mirror. In fact, many of us are so busy trying to measure up to unrealistic expectations that we don't even realize that what feels like an insurmountable wall is actually a door we can open and walk through. When we do—by asking questions, putting our less-than-perfect ideas forward,

Women face a powerful barrier that we must break through to make it to bigger leadership roles. It is not the glass ceiling— it is the mirrored door.

speaking up for ourselves and what we want, and more that we will discuss in the coming pages—we strengthen our position. Through risk-taking and the rewards of lessons learned, we truly become ready, but that is on the other side of the threshold. When we step forward and enter the room, we can have a seat at the table of decisions and impact.

All too often, we are waiting—in the wings, for our turn, for someone to notice us and our hard work. This waiting casts us as the supporting player, playing small, rather than as the lead in our story. It quiets that little voice, that inner knowing that tells us we can be so much more.

What We Learned

How did we get here? It starts early. In school, girls are rewarded for getting As, for modesty, polite behavior, and being the good girls who fit in and don't make a fuss. Role models in real life and in media reinforce this behavior. Societal messages dictate how women should look, which can be especially difficult for women of color and people from other underrepresented groups. Girls observe these signs and wonder if they measure up to this ideal. They begin to feel less than, not worthy, and the need to work twice as hard for half as much.

We learned in school to follow the rules, have the answers ready, and be polite and well-behaved. While the boys had a greater range of expected behavior, our teachers needed and counted on us to be model students with exemplary conduct. It worked for us, and we relished the role. It brought tears sometimes, when we didn't get the grade or were reprimanded, as we became more and more invested in others' opinions and validation of us.

In past generations, women were protected, provided for, and put on a pedestal. In a world where men worked and women took care of the house and home, this was the norm. Today, most adult women work outside the home. Households look nothing like the past, economics indicate the importance and necessity of women working, and careers no longer include a lifetime at one company. Those earlier societal norms no longer serve today's times, and they haven't in decades. Yet, they are still part of the underlying culture and conditioning, setting up absurd expectations, particularly for women. This contributes to us believing that perfection is our price of admission.

Here is the paradox: We hate the unrealistic expectations embedded in our culture (and in our own minds), yet we contribute to them by being on a perfection treadmill, showing a perfect self to the world, and waiting for the "right" answer, the "right" time, and the "right" place to show up at our best. We are hiding our perfectly imperfect, authentic self and real opinions from the world that needs us as we are. Isn't it time we come clean and show up without all the right answers? Isn't it time we encourage each other to do the same and show future generations of girls and women that they are okay just as they are? What would life be like if we took more leaps, believed we were ready enough, and became more at ease with not having all the answers? What if we chose progress over perfection?

How We Hold Ourselves Back

Perfectionism is increasing over time, cites a study by Thomas Curran and Andrew P. Hill. Through psychological testing, they discovered that between 1989 and 2016, American, Canadian, and British college students' levels of self-oriented, socially prescribed, and "other"-oriented (putting others first) perfectionism increased by "statistically significant amounts." Young people are more demanding of themselves, perceive that others are more demanding of them, and are more demanding of others.

The costs of perfection are beyond inaction and hesitancy. Multiple research studies indicate an increase in stress, burnout, workaholism, anxiety, and depression. While perfectionists may be more motivated and conscientious, and may deliver higher-quality work than non-perfectionists, there is a significant downside. Their excessively high standards lead to all-or-nothing behavior and believing their self-worth is dependent on perfection.

A commonly referred to Hewlett-Packard study showed that women are less likely to apply for or pursue jobs or promotions unless they have 100 percent of the company's stated criteria. Men see the criteria as a wish list and, with strong self-belief and a greater inclination to take risks, apply for new roles with only about 60 percent of the skills required. Their increased attempts and more positive self-perception lead to more promotions and upward movement in their careers, not to mention swagger that becomes a self-fulfilling prophecy.

Still so much of the focus in popular women's leadership press is on leaning in early and then cracking the top barrier of the glass ceiling later in their careers. There is so much more that we can learn from and address in the years in between.

"Our beliefs in ourselves are important in shaping all kinds of important decisions, such as what colleges we apply to, which career paths we choose, and whether we are willing to contribute ideas in the workplace or try to compete for a promotion," says Harvard Business School associate professor Katherine B. Coffman. In her research, she found that gender stereotypes distort our views of others and ourselves. When we buy into these stereotypes, we see ourselves through a critical lens, despite having the skills to succeed. The result can lead to lower confidence, a habit of discounting positive feedback, and less willingness to express ideas or speak up in groups. We downplay ourselves and deny our teams our valuable contributions. This dynamic should be a rallying cry for organizations to create a different environment and way of working that challenges stereotypes and enables women to thrive.

I've now instituted women's welcome events adjacent to our MBA orientation. These are designed to increase belonging, connection, and confidence. We share the research, reinforce how much we need the students' contributions, and encourage them to raise their hands, find their voice, and lead in the classroom, in extracurricular activities, and in their lives. I share my story of arriving in the program and my own wonder about an admissions mistake. When my story resonates, I see the sense of familiarity and relief on their faces, hear the knowing laughter of self-recognition, and watch their bodies relax. When we share our stories and the facts, we show girls and women they are not alone. We validate that this conditioning is not our fault, is all too common, and can be unlearned with conscious effort, some risk-taking, and determination.

You may be thinking this leads to yet another burden on women. To be sure, undoing years of embedded learning is hard work. However, the snail's pace of change in corporations and government policies leads me to believe that the change needs to start with us. Why wait for organizations to reset when the clear path within our control is to free ourselves from stereotypical messages and ways of being? When we recognize and question our past patterns, we can open the discussion for the future. We can show the girls and women behind us and the boys and men beside us a new way for all.

Raise Your Future

My client Michelle continued to strive for the CMO job. As we dug deeper through our work together, she recognized that she was perpetually perfecting presentations, analyses, and message points but not engaging in debate, especially with her boss. She orchestrated thoughtful work that had value, for sure. But she was regularly disappointed when her proposals were not approved as they were and her hard work was not acknowledged.

· When we discussed the unspoken rules of success she held for herself, she realized that one was to make her boss look good. This advice had served her well in her first job, so she never disagreed with her current boss and always ensured things went as planned, with no surprises. Fifteen years later, this thinking led her to downplay herself and avoid taking risks that might tarnish her dependable, loyal image. She connected these habits to his feedback that she should express a stronger point of view, be more open to new ideas from others, and take a stronger lead in the discussions.

When Michelle identified the gap between her intentions and her impact, she saw her actions in a new light. Her past focus on control and preparation led her to play it safe. She had previously avoided and then felt locked out of high risk/reward interactions where ideas were critiqued and decisions made. She knew she could make a difference, recognized she was blocking herself, and was finally determined to take more risks.

Committed to a new approach, she psyched herself up and prepped differently to take a greater role in important debates. She realized that given her knowledge and expertise, the presence they wanted from her was to influence the discussions, help solve the conflicts, and be a key part of the collaborations. She forced herself to take a stand even when it included disagreement with her boss. She let go of feeling that she had to please him, save face, and show up perfectly. She walked through the mirrored door and was involved in a new way.

We identified small steps for her to take to create and participate in these discussions in the face of her fear. The more she did it, the easier it became. She was back to feeling like a player that mattered. She stopped expecting that she would finally be noticed. She began to feel more confident and clearer about what she wanted at the company and how she wanted to work. In time, Michelle realized she wasn't willing to wait for the CMO job she wanted. Soon after that, she accepted an outside offer. She had learned to be quicker to interact, to take more chances, and that she is usually ready enough to raise her opinions.

We fool ourselves into believing that perfection is the price of admission to business school, the C-suite, or whatever we want from others or in our future. We work way too hard to let this thinking or these well-intended, out-of-date messages get in our own way. When we break through the mirrored door, we gain lessons from success and failure. We take risks and reap the rewards of being in the action. In doing so, we create momentum for our own development and a brighter future.

The Time Is Now

This book is a road map to enlighten and encourage you to open the mirrored door and pass over the threshold to your future. The first step is to grant yourself permission to explore. I encourage you to allow yourself the time and space to become more self-aware, take chances, and get inspired for your journey. You may feel daunted by the magnitude of stepping into a new way. Maybe you need more than a permission slip and want a hall pass as you venture outside of your familiar place. You want it, you got it! Join me as we uncover the tales we tell ourselves, discover areas to let go, and experiment and explore all we can be.

To get started, I invite you to consider your typical mindset and likelihood to act or hesitate when there is an opportunity to raise your hand in some part of your life. What doorway can you walk through to move into action and growth? Is there a particular situation or place that triggers hesitation? What small act of courage can you take in the next week? Perhaps it is completing an application to lead a project or for a new job you don't feel 100 percent ready for. Maybe it's sharing your opinion on the future of your company or team. Is it the introduction you have wanted but thought it was too pushy to request? Perhaps it's seeking the support you need to take care of yourself in some new way. As you take this risk, consider what you may learn from doing it. Focus not on success or failure but on what you will gain in the experience of putting yourself out there. Where are you ready enough to open the mirrored door?

KEY TAKEAWAYS

- High-achieving women have a track record of success in school and in early careers fueled by hard work, preparation, and the ability to deliver.

- As our careers grow, the expectations change and sometimes conflict with the early markers of achievement that were embedded in our identities.

- The mirrored door is when we face opportunity and hesitate, questioning our readiness or worthiness. We do what has worked before and come up short against new expectations of risk-taking, conflict management, decision-making, and negotiations.

- The mirrored door shows us what we often sense when feeling stalled or stifled. We may be locked out by systemic issues but may also inadvertently be locking ourselves in.

JOURNAL PROMPTS

- When presented with a new opportunity, how do you usually respond?

- Describe your current career outlook and momentum. What's most in your favor and most in your way?

- What's one small step you can take this week? (Refer to the last paragraph of this chapter for ideas.)

I'm glad you are here. You can do this. Let's get to work!

Looking Back
to Move Forward

. . . .

"Sugar and spice and everything nice;
that's what little girls are made of."
ATTRIBUTED TO ROBERT SOUTHEY

"**Y**OU ARE not gonna believe it. Mrs. Munch wrote Allie's name on the whiteboard today!" Katie said breathlessly at our dinner table. My husband's and my limited reaction to this breaking news seemed to frustrate my daughter as she looked at us incredulously and put down her turkey taco. "That means her conduct was unacceptable and will not be tolerated," she said with a knowing tone.

Still not provoking the reaction she hoped for, Katie raised her high-pitched voice with grave concern and said, "She's the first girl on the board. *Ever!*" After a pause, she added, "Allie wasn't supposed to question the assignments." Her voice trailed off and she quietly settled into a thoughtful gaze, likely pondering the new world order of her fourth-grade class.

And so it begins.

This elementary school scandal upended Katie's underlying beliefs: Girls don't act out. Girls don't cause trouble. Girls stay quiet and obedient and get rewarded for it. She learned a new lesson that day—acting out was especially bad for a girl. While good-girl behavior serves us well in many ways, these early lessons seed our roles as the well-behaved ones, the peacemakers, the ones who comply and avoid risks. It takes most of us years to realize that risk-taking and questioning and breaking the rules can build our leadership and self-advocacy. Case in point: Allie now acts out at an Ivy League school, playing on the varsity soccer team.

I recall an afternoon when I was a few years older than Katie. I was thrilled to be included in a neighborhood baseball game with my three older brothers. In the preceding years, I had felt like one of the boys, but our time playing together had faded when I became a tween. That day, I savored every minute of play.

The fun ended, though, when an outraged boy named Timmy quit the game in disagreement once he was called out unanimously. In his frustration, he took his equipment but didn't go home. He stayed on the side watching with a sneer on his face and his pricey bat and ball in hand. We continued playing with our battered equipment, including a tennis ball, which enabled far bigger hits and many home runs.

I relished my triple, then waited on base. There were two outs and the game was tied in our final inning. My brothers egged me on to steal home base and win the game. When the batter connected, I took off, driven to be the victor and to show Timmy that his stunt hadn't stopped the game.

On my *Chariots of Fire* run to home, Timmy blocked my way with his arms up like a football player. I couldn't get around him. I didn't know what to do. I had to make it to home base. Completely out of character, I matched his middle-school anger with my own. I punched him and ran to the plate, ending the game as my brothers cheered our victory. I delighted in their pride and shock that I stood up to Timmy's unsportsmanlike behavior, making that run worth more to me than the win. I was on a higher plane with my newly earned respect and sudden sense that I was finally part of their group again.

When I returned home, though, my pride was cut short. I knew from my mom's serious expression and the sway of the dangling telephone cord that she had just hung up with Timmy's mom. I was in trouble. With a disappointed look in her eyes, she said firmly, "A young lady doesn't fight."

This was one more lesson in how I was to act in the world. I was supposed to go along to get along. Even when blocked or treated unfairly, I should be nice to the Timmys of the world.

Our education starts early. We are conditioned to be nice, likeable, helpful, non-combative, and pleasing. It is part of the fabric of girls' upbringing and women's lives. We learn the roles that we should play from our well-intentioned families, schools, and communities. The workplace validates these expectations as we find ourselves under a microscope that evaluates how we show up to and for others.

Ingrained Biases

My client Samantha was exasperated by the guidance she had received from her boss. During her performance review, he had advised her to build stronger ties with her colleagues—and told her she needed to smile more.

As a senior manager at a consulting firm, Samantha excelled at getting to the root of problems and quickly figuring out options to resolve issues. In her twenties, to be seen as more mature, she learned to convey seriousness when she managed projects and others. She was rewarded for this adaptation with promotions and outstanding performance reviews. This new feedback threw her off balance and seemed to counter what worked for her as she built her credibility and her career.

After reflecting on the last six months, she came to me and asked, "Why do I have to be the one to smile? Would they have ever said that to a man?"

"Probably not," I replied. "Still, there is more to understand about this comment."

Samantha may have been facing a double bind of gendered expectations: When women take charge, they are viewed as competent leaders but are seen as less likeable. Conversely, when women take care, they are viewed as warm but less competent. Because of this dynamic, women constantly need to prove themselves against a higher bar of competence while also managing the biased perceptions of others. In my younger days, I was seen as smiling too much. When I got more focused and serious, all too often people would ask me, "Are you okay?" Concern subsided when I explained that nothing was wrong and that I was eager to jump into the discussion.

To Samantha, I offered, "What matters now is to learn more and understand the perception others have. Are you seen as intimidating, unengaged, or unhappy with your team or job? Said another way, how is your smiling, or not, impacting your relationships and work? Are people uncomfortable, scared of you, or simply not used to a woman getting down to business? When you learn more, consider what you might want to change, if anything. What might you share, point out, or ask of others? Does the comment open a conversation on areas of dissatisfaction? Getting more detail can lead to more discussion."

Our society's ingrained biases of women's facial expressions make them open to interpretation, whether we like it or not. For those who think this is a thing of the past, consider the more recent term "resting bitch face" and how people use it primarily to describe women. Research has found that if women don't exhibit warm nonverbal communication, they are viewed more harshly. The opportunity for leaders is to redefine what leadership looks like. To disrupt the current state, we need the courage to call out feedback based on stereotypes, a more thoughtful and actionable approach to performance review feedback, and a reconsideration of the standards to which we hold others.

Expected Roles

After a three-year stint as chief of staff to the CEO, Micah was ready to make a bigger impact as the newly promoted division president. Following her promotion, she was eager to finally attend the C-suite retreat as a participant rather than in the planning role she had played previously. She would be the only woman among her peers in the room, but she commanded a significant part of the business. This gave her a sense of confidence about her new seat at the table.

On day one, when the brainstorming began, the CEO asked Micah to be the scribe. In that moment, her excitement plummeted. Did he see her in her old role, always willing to help? Had he asked her male peers to do this in past meetings? She agreed to take notes and instantly regretted it. Should she have said no and possibly damaged her reputation or, even worse, limited her career? Could she have said yes and then asked someone else to be the scribe the next morning? Eventually, she talked to her boss about the situation.

"It was a blind spot," he told her. "You are always ready to help. I thought you would want to take notes because you are so good at it."

Ugh! Micah thought, but she stayed quiet. In her new role, she needed to be seen as a peer to those at the table, not as the support staff "handling the office housework," as she later put it to me.

When I was a young sales manager, I was part of a robust training program that taught me how to sell and how to manage other people. I was fortunate, but along with it came advice about how to show up and look professional. As one of the only women in the region and the only female district manager, I was set up to be a role model. We were all advised to wear navy jackets to the regional meetings. I wore a red jacket instead.

My well-intentioned boss asked me a series of questions to show me that this was the wrong way to stand out. To continue to climb the ladder, I complied; yet, over time, I felt as though I was playing someone else's game. The rules seemed to be telling me to act like one of the guys, or at the very least to dress like one. This, at a time when women were new to the company and to the business world. I learned to give a hearty handshake and adopt a game face to cover up my expressive face, and that my naturally lower voice and five-foot-seven height (considered tall then) was an advantage. My in-depth knowledge of Southeastern College football and experience talking sports with my brothers served me well as I moved through Florida, Tennessee, and Georgia.

Once I moved to our headquarters in Chicago, I saw more women in brand management, and they dressed professionally yet in a more feminine style. I began to feel that my leadership development to date had included making me something that I was not. As though I were playing Twister, I was contorting myself in awkward, unnatural ways that had me near collapse. I valued my mentors and managers and know now that they were doing the best they could in a changing world.

Biases are so ingrained that we don't see them much of the time. Through reflection and training, we can identify the biases and rules in our subconscious. Many times, bias is good and helps us navigate life. When we prejudge that the stove might be hot or that it's not a great idea to take the shortcut through a dark alley, both help us make good choices. But bias goes wrong when we limit ourselves or others limit us without realizing it.

We all have biases. They can put us in a box, and that box is smaller for women. Women face the expectation of warmth. Men face the expectation of competence, which is why we so easily imagine a man when we think of a leader. When men are also warm, it is a bonus, as long as they are competent. But we are not socialized to expect a competent woman in the work-place, especially if she leads with competence. And when we don't see warmth in a woman, it triggers a red flag. For exam-ple, sometimes when a woman gets down to business right away, she disrupts the image of what a woman is supposed to do or be. She is supposed to be nice, friendly, warm. She is sup-posed to make sure everyone in the conversation is okay. She is supposed to pick up on and address the environment. She is supposed to take notes, refresh the beverages, clear the table, follow up, and above all else, smile.

Although there is much to be done to address the biases we face from others in the workplace, I believe that we are biased against ourselves too. We have rules about what we can and can't do that stem from our conditioning, such as growing up to look pretty, avoid risks, be perfect, always comply, and be a helper. Then when we newly take a big risk and/or help our-selves, we feel fear and/or guilt. Although we may face a greater penalty than a man would for the novel behavior, sometimes our own concerns immobilize us. We don't step into new situ-ations that could lead to greater personal development and a brighter future.

We all have biases. They can put us in a box, and that box is smaller for women.

Communication Norms

One of the most impactful things we learn as children is how to communicate with each other. Deborah Tannen, a professor of linguistics at Georgetown University and bestselling author of *You Just Don't Understand! Women and Men in Conversation*, found that because of our tendency as youth to play with people of the same gender, the lessons we learn vary greatly.

When she studied organizations, Tannen found that those early relationship behaviors stay with us into adulthood and the workplace. When she analyzed conversational styles between girls and boys in the United States, she saw that girls connect by building rapport, and boys by showing status. Tannen observed that among girls, small group interactions, lots of talking, and secret-telling establish closeness. Girls also learn what not to do. They downplay strengths to convey they are the same. They limit sounding too sure or certain and minimize accomplishments to avoid becoming unpopular. The fear of being criticized or cast off from the group leads them to prioritize others' needs above their own and keep the peace. They strive for ways to build connection with each other.

Boys operate very differently: in larger groups, stratifying by status, interests, and skills. Those with high status elevate themselves, one-up others, and emerge as leaders. Boys are incented to show their achievements and knowledge. The group members encourage one another to lead with stories and jokes to heighten their standing. They learn to challenge each other to negotiate their rank in the hierarchy. When they do, they tell low-status boys what to do with no worry of being called "bossy." Their fear is losing face in the one-up, one-down dynamic.

While all genders communicate with both cooperation and competition, Tannen states that girls prioritize cooperation and connection, and boys prioritize competition and status. While these findings may not be true of all childhood socialization, linguists found similar results across genders regardless of culture. When I share this research in my coaching or keynotes, I see nods of recognition. Though neither approach is right or wrong, the lived experience that matches Tannen's work shows how and why we may struggle in the workplace based on what we've learned and expect of each other. It can feel as though men and women are from different planets, as the aptly named book *Men Are from Mars, Women Are from Venus* revealed in the 1990s. With women's value of cooperation in communication and men's in competition, it's not surprising that in the workplace women 1) find their ideas taken by and credited to someone else, 2) are often interrupted or talked over, and/or 3) feel they are steamrolled into agreement. If men learned to downplay doubt to avoid the appearance of weakness and women learned to downplay certainty to avoid sounding superior, we collectively need to find a middle ground to let go of the chains of the past and better manage risk in our companies.

Tannen's research teaches us to assume positive intent, and that it's not our fault—we did the best we could with the norms of the day. Perhaps the meeting dynamics that can lead to frustration truly stem from our collective conditioned communications styles more than from bad intentions. We may seem as though we are from different planets, but it is time we find our way together.

Changing Roles

I remember a perfume ad on TV in the '80s that was lodged in my head due to the irritating yet catchy jingle. The message broke the mold of women's roles at a time when women were beginning to enter the workplace in greater numbers. A sexy, confident woman sang, "I can bring home the bacon, fry it up in a pan, and never let you forget you're a man," while casually spritzing perfume on herself in different work and home outfits. This was the first time I equated a woman's success with the "you can do it all" message that has been so challenging to live up to for most women.

Still, things seemed to be changing. As women gained independence through work, a wave of movies and TV shows, like *An Unmarried Woman* and *One Day at a Time*, featured single moms. I recall the news that a neighbor's parents were getting a divorce. These announcements increased in those days and were usually shared in the hushed tone of a cancer diagnosis. There was never a congratulations or consideration that maybe this was a good thing given their unique situation. I learned another rule: being married equaled success. Single, unmarried, or divorced was not what you wanted to be. In 1986, *Newsweek* validated this belief when the publication shared a report that single women in their thirties had a 20 percent chance of getting married and those over forty had a greater chance of being killed by a terrorist than getting married. It seemed women's successes were tied to our relationships with men.

The reality was that this new way for women was built on a huge foundation of societal norms for American/Western women. Having it all meant taking on the roles of my mother and my father, but as one person, and with just twenty-four hours a day. That brand of perfume left store shelves decades ago, but the tug between assuming traditional women's roles and the "take charge" directive for today's young women is still front and center.

Gendered Expectations

During her *Lean In* book tour, Sheryl Sandberg suggested we stop calling girls "bossy" and instead compliment their leaderships skills. We raise our girls to be good, safe, model citizens, then wonder why women struggle sometimes to claim their voice, set boundaries, prioritize themselves, and take the lead.

Our conditioning makes us empathetic leaders who can read a room and manage everyone else's emotions, happiness, and satisfaction. Although families, workplaces, and communities need our agility, relational awareness, emotional intelligence, and experience in defusing conflict, this dynamic can be exhausting. Focused on everyone else, we are zapped of energy and over time may neglect our own needs and wants. We submerge what we want and who we are for the sake of others' opinions.

We face the mirrored door when our educational readiness and career ambitions meet the gendered expectations planted in our minds and the perceptions that surround us. Too many well-equipped women reflect inward and hesitate or procrastinate instead of risking action. The power of looking back on how we got here is that it can inform how we move forward.

Our conditioned socialization to be "other"-oriented and look for affirmation is a double-edged sword. It gives us many great gifts like consensus- and connection-building, risk avoidance, and care for the greater good. These "softer skills" historically have not been priorities in organizations, but they have grown in importance to meet the needs of the changing marketplace and workforce.

Our socialization came with the territory of our gender and is not our fault. We could commiserate about the masculine traits that may not have been taught to us and yet have been the heritage of corporate leadership. Our energy, however, is best spent on what we can do to accept the past and carry forward with what we need now in our careers and lives. We are where we are. To be sure, there are some habits to let go of and some to learn. So now what? If we perpetuate the past conditioning that limits us, we have no chance to drive the change we want, the self we want to prioritize, and the future we want for the girls and women of the world.

Women on the Brink

When I was in middle school in the mid-1970s, my big sister came home from college and gave me a T-shirt that read: "A Woman's Place is in the House... and the Senate." It quickly became my prized possession. The gift symbolized something important to me, as it bridged our seven-year age gap and somehow linked my skinny tween self to adult women. I doubt that I fully understood the magnitude of the shirt's statement back then, but I wore it proudly and far too frequently. It felt to me that girls and women were on the brink of something big. I loved the sense that the future looked bright, and I wanted to be part of it. Fast-forward several decades, and more women lead countries around the world and run for political office now than at any other time in our history.

But the sad stats on women's representation in company leadership tell us we have much work to do. According to the 2022 *Women in the Workplace* study by McKinsey and LeanIn.Org, women represent 48 percent of entry-level employees and just 26 percent of the C-suite. The numbers for women of color are worse, at 19 percent and 5 percent, respectively. Still, my hopes are high. I see the "no, thank you" evaluation women have made about many employers when faced with the COVID-induced, more visible strain of work and life demands. I'm inspired by Gen Z's quest for values, purpose, and balance in their work that has caught the attention of employers. I'm encouraged by investors setting guidelines for diversity, sustainability, and a broader definition of company stakeholders to include employees, customers, communities, and the environment. I am a part of boardroom discussions to combat findings, like those in the *Women in the Workplace 2022* report, that women gain far fewer of the all-important first-time manager-level positions than men. I value the research that enlightens companies to create inclusion, psychological safety, and belonging beyond the numbers. These advancements collide with the heartbreakingly glacial pace of women's advancement, creating a possibility to turn disappointment and delays into determination and difference-making.

While we still face so much darkness, I see light. Maybe we are on the brink of a new dawn. We can answer the call to face the challenges the past has bestowed on us in the present and drive the change we need for the future. Join me as we cocreate a new path forward.

KEY TAKEAWAYS

- Biases are informed by many influences, including our upbringing, culture, family, and education. They can lead to expectations that limit opportunities, authenticity, roles, behavior, and potential.

- Girls and boys are socialized to communicate differently. Girls learn to connect with each other and downplay certainty and superiority. Boys learn to "fake it till you make it" with more ease. This learned behavior stays with us as adults.

- Girls learn that prioritizing others' opinions can lead to affirmation, acceptance, reduced risk, approval, and likeability. It also enables them to empathize and become skillfully aware of others' reactions.

- In the workplace setting, women are expected to show "other"-oriented warmth while also exhibiting stereotypically masculine, take-charge leadership behavior. This is a double bind in which women may face backlash and be seen as too soft or too tough, but never just right.

JOURNAL PROMPTS

- What did success look like for you growing up? How did those around you define success? How were you treated, rewarded, noticed?

- What were the unwritten rules of friendships and other relationships?

- What themes of your upbringing stay with you now?

3

The Mirrored Maze of Work

. . . .

"Careers are a jungle gym, not a ladder."
SHERYL SANDBERG

"**I**'M READY TO PLAY!**" I proclaimed as the door slammed behind me. Outside, the cars were parked to provide clearance to our front yard basketball court for the upcoming game. There was extra space for my brothers' running leaps and lunges that kept the ball in bounds.

Fortunately, I made my announcement before the sides were picked. I hoped to get on a good team, where they'd pass me the ball. I had practiced my three-point shots endlessly because I knew the boys wouldn't cover me so far from the basket.

In reaction to my announcement, faces froze. Everyone suddenly stood still as statues. The warm-up shots ended as multiple basketballs dropped to the pavement. *Bounce. Bounce. Bounce.* No one would look directly at me. *Bounce. Bounce.* They whispered under their breath. Time seemed to pause.

"Ellen, you're not going to be able to play today. We have an even number already," my dad finally said as a younger neighbor walked up the driveway.

I wondered if I heard him correctly. My jaw tightened. I stood there stone-faced and silent while a familiar flush spread across my face and neck. Minutes later, I ran inside to wipe my burning eyes and saw my pink-polished fingernail clippings in the bathroom trash can.

"You'll scratch the boys if you play," I was warned earlier when we were deciding to play that afternoon. I had solved that problem, or so I thought.

In all candor, I really wasn't sure I wanted to share this story of my beloved father, who told me I could do anything I set my mind to. My brothers, who were young teens back then, have always been some of my biggest supporters. I'd like to simply erase this memory. At the time, I told myself that's just the way it was. Oddly enough, none of them remember it, but my younger sister and I sure do.

"You are including the time you cut off your nails, right?" my sister assumed when I told her about my book. "You always had such long, polished nails back then. You were so mad."

She was right. It was my first little heartbreak and entry into a world that was built for others, not for me. I was confused and wondered why the rules had changed. I didn't know why I had so suddenly been excluded, as if a "no girls allowed" sign had been placed on the basketball hoop. In hindsight, I learned that even when girls or women follow the prescribed rules, we can still be locked out. I realized what no one says aloud—that I didn't belong or should choose other places. And hardest of all, I learned that our heroes and mentors can sometimes let us down as they unwittingly keep up the status quo.

This day probably motivated me to prove myself, show up, and hold my own with the guys in other venues. It highlighted the resilience I'd need to enter places where I was the only woman and didn't know the unspoken rules. It was clear they didn't expect me on their turf and thought I should already know that. With the advancements of Title IX, the law intended to equalize opportunities for girls, and the expansive availability of girls' sports, you are probably thinking we've moved beyond stories like this. Or have we? Maybe this story is not about basketball at all.

A World Built for the Past

Let's fast-forward to today's rapidly changing workplace, where we are all trying to find our way, regardless of our gender, race, culture, sexual orientation, age, religion, or ability. In the workplace, some navigate this tough terrain without the benefit of advice from parental role models, without senior leaders who look like us, and without the road maps that others seem to have at the ready. Those newer to the party may feel like outsiders as they pioneer a path for many.

Whether you are trying to advance your own career or be a champion for others to do the same, I invite you to think about the path ahead with the eyes of a traveler. Bring along your curiosity. The journey is long and there will be delays and cancellations, as well as sites to behold and people and places that transform us. Let this chapter serve as a trip advisor of sorts as we review the culture, language, and things to do to extend and enjoy your stay.

The numbers speak for themselves—we collectively have a lot of work to do. While women make up the majority of valedictorians, college graduates, and entry-level roles, their career advancement ends early. Men gain 62 percent of first-time manager positions, and women, 38 percent. The McKinsey–LeanIn.Org *Women in the Workplace 2022* study mentioned in chapter 2 refers to that gap as the "broken rung." Women run just 4.8 percent of the Fortune Global 500 companies.

Fewer women make it to the C-suite, and of the two thousand newest US companies that have gone public, only eighteen had female founders. Statistics also show us that the global pay gap persists, with women making 77 cents for every dollar men make, according to the United Nations. In 2020, the US numbers looked better, with women earning 88 cents on men's dollar, and with an encouraging sign that women ages twenty-five to thirty-four earned 93 cents compared to men of the same age group. Yet data also shows that on average, Black women in the United States are paid 36 percent less than white men and 12 percent less than white women. We can celebrate small amounts of progress and still see that we've got so much more to do. At the current rate, the UN report indicates, it will take 257 years to close the global gender pay gap.

The professional white-collar workplace in many, if not most, organizations is an updated version of the 1950s workplace. This was by and large all-white, all-male, and nine-to-five. Today, the workplace is more diverse than at any time in history regarding gender, race, culture, religion, and a workforce that spans four generations. This massive change took place in sixty to seventy years, which is a short time frame in the big scheme of history. While HR manuals have been updated to serve a different worker and newer laws, the mechanics of work are still rooted in the past. Still, marveling at how major historical shifts took place so quickly provides no comfort as we struggle with outdated perceptions, leadership identity, and communication styles.

Performance and Perceptions

"You need to work on your stand-up leadership skills. And I think I can help." I recall my boss Chuck Maniscalco saying this to me at the end of a glowing performance review.

The rest of the conversation went something like this:

"Sounds good. Do you mean I need to work on my presentation skills?"

"Not exactly... Well, yes, but that is not all. You need to convey stand-up leadership skills."

"I'm not sure I know what that means. Is it how I present in front of a large group?" I tried again.

"It's about projecting a stronger... I don't know... presence. We'll continue to talk about it in our weekly one-on-ones."

With that, Chuck checked his watch and closed his portfolio.

The only thing clear to me was that the meeting was over. I respected Chuck and knew he believed in me. But something about his comments and lack of ease seemed unusual. He was a thoughtful and amazing boss, but somehow not in the final minutes of my performance review. I left feeling caught off guard and worried about my future. I was a marketing director striving to become a vice president at Quaker Oats. My scope of business was comparable to that of a VP. I prided myself on being Chuck's go-to person. I felt I was doing the job of a VP, but I didn't have the title yet. Senior management seemed to bet on my peers succeeding at the next level, whereas I needed to prove myself again and again.

One year earlier, Chuck had shown he believed in me and advocated for me when my job was on the line. When the company announced that several director roles would be eliminated, I was desperate to stay, and after learning that our division would go from two to only one director, I was nervous about my chances. I was an underdog, having transferred from sales to brand management and marketing. My background was more eclectic relative to my peers who had joined the company from prestigious full-time MBA programs and universities. I had earned my MBA from Kellogg while working full time, making me late to the brand function and less connected to all the other marketers in the company. And I was pregnant, which was not ideal when they were looking to reduce head count. Still, I told myself that my sales background was an asset in leading cross-functional teams, especially given upcoming product launches. I was so eager and determined that in a small act of courage, I shared with Chuck how much I wanted the director job and a long-term career at the company. I laid out why I thought I was the one for the business and how I'd handle my leave.

"I am surprised. With so much about to change for you, I thought you weren't sure," he responded. "I'm glad you told me."

After having babies, most women at this company returned to part-time roles or not at all, but I thought he knew I was different. In my mind, I showed no hesitancy.

"I plan to be a working mom and want to do that here," I said with determination. "I think I'm the right person for what our division needs now," I added, along with my rationale. As I left, I said, "I will support whatever you decide. And if you choose me, I promise, you won't regret it."

After a stressful wait, I was elated to find out that he had picked me as his director. While I knew I wanted it more than his alternative, I was somewhat surprised that I had been chosen over my peer, who had a more typical background for the role. I was glad I'd told Chuck how much I wanted the role, and affirmed my intention to return after my first daughter was born.

Mirrors in the Maze

Being chosen by Chuck when he could have eliminated my job a year earlier initially led me to believe that he had my back and was figuring out how to help me with my career. Even though he had fumbled during this latest feedback, I trusted in his support. But I soon started to question whether he truly thought I was VP material, whether that odd performance discussion signaled that Chuck regretted choosing me. I couldn't shake this idea that I had let him down. Our usual one-on-one time became more formal and infrequent. It got the best of me. I overthought what I did in every interaction and at each meeting. Several times in group meetings, he would respond to my comments by opening his mouth to speak and then, instead, pursing his lips. I racked my brain wondering what he wanted to say. I became more self-critical and feared my precious career was slipping through my hands. I told myself that my days were numbered. Although I didn't think of it this way at the time, it was like walking through a maze and encountering the mirrored door at every turn.

I asked my mentoring circle for help. I counted on this peer-led group of women in my company for career advice and intel, and as a sounding board. When I asked about "stand-up leadership skills," I was met with blank stares. No one had heard that term. As we discussed performance reviews, each woman shared that she had received some form of feedback regarding her style, presence, gravitas, what others thought, or the way she dealt with conflict. It seemed as if we were all being told we were either too quiet or too loud, too hesitant or too overbearing, too this or too that. I wondered why none of the ten of us high-potential women was deemed just right. Worse yet, we obsessed over the negative feedback instead of all the positives. Still, no one could decipher what stand-up leadership truly was.

I summoned my courage yet again to clarify where I stood with Chuck and to understand the perceptions of the unnamed deciders of my future. I asked him every chance I got and was promptly brushed off because of his schedule. It became a wedge between us, and I began to wonder if I could trust him.

Perhaps my career was washed up, he couldn't bring himself to tell me, and it was time to look externally for another job.

In my frustration, one day I finally said to him, "I ask myself daily: Should I stay or should I go?"

Chuck's eyes widened. "We want you here. There are simply some things for you to work on, especially in front of senior leadership. We need to showcase you," he said, looking directly at me.

"'Showcase me,'" I replied with air quotes. I shrugged and threw my hands up and pleaded, "Just tell me, what's going on? Did I do something wrong?"

There was a long pause. He started to speak then stopped, several times. Finally, he blurted out with a gasp, "The senior leaders think you aren't tough enough. I know you are because I see you in action every day, but it's not how you show up with them. It's why they aren't sure you are VP ready..." His voice trailed off.

I was crushed. I had logged endless hours and delivered double-digit growth. I thought that was enough for me to be seen. I was shocked that I had to jump through more hoops.

"I lead a portfolio of brands of over half a billion dollars. I manage multiple teams of people and received some of the strongest 360-degree feedback reviews. You know I run circles around some of my peers who have already been promoted to VP. This is the view from senior leaders who only see me once a quarter. How is that fair?" I asked with a sharp tone that I instantly regretted. I knew Chuck well enough to talk straight and confide in him, but I'd never blamed him or got angry with him before that day.

"Ellen, every interaction matters, including this one," he said. "You have to admit that you clam up in those quarterly meetings. As you said, they don't get a chance to see you often. I pushed and pushed for your promotion, but unfortunately it didn't happen this time."

"Well, I'm glad I know where I stand," I muttered. I picked up my pad and stormed out of his office.

In the mirrored maze,
we face the mirrored
door again and again.
We question ourselves,
think we are alone, and
take the blame personally.

My eyes welled up and, in a flash, I knew he was right. I was pleasant but quiet in the strategic and operating plan meetings with the CEO and his team. To avoid saying something wrong, I said the minimum needed. If they weighed these interactions above the numbers and Chuck's word, of course they wouldn't think I was leadership material. I figured I might be finished there and thought it was time to update my résumé. How had I let this happen?

While this occurred decades ago, I continue to hear eerily similar stories from clients, friends, and women in my courses and retreats. They usually have a track record of success, a do-what-it-takes attitude, and strong relationships within their teams, and then suddenly they have a lower rating, miss a promotion, or get an unfavorable assignment that comes as a complete surprise. And this frequently happens to insightful, observant women who pick up on the nuances of the dynamics around them. What drives these circumstances, and how have they not been solved yet? How can we avoid this happening to the younger women emerging behind us? How do we see it coming, and how can we stop it before it happens?

Women are well-versed in the glass ceiling, the metaphorical obstruction that holds us back at the top of an organization. We now have the broken rung showing women underrepresented at the position of first-time manager. Clearly, a lot is happening between the broken rung and the glass ceiling for women who aspire to lead.

Alice Eagly and Linda Carli describe a woman's career path as a labyrinth to symbolize the systemic obstacles we navigate and that men don't face. This powerful metaphor acknowledges the slow but improving access to leadership for women over the last several decades, the potential to arrive at the center, and the multiple blockades we face throughout our careers. Eagly and Carli cite gender stereotypes that limit leadership perceptions of women, discrimination in promotion and pay, less access to mentors and networks, and the over-indexing of domestic responsibilities as the top challenges unique to women. The labyrinth reflects a journey of twists and turns, dead ends, and detours, and, through resilience, hard-earned rewards.

The unforeseen complexities and confusion can lead us to doubt the systems and culture. Eagly and Carli call this a labyrinth; I call it a mirrored maze because in it we face the mirrored door again and again. We question ourselves, think we are alone, and take the blame personally.

I had thought the path was clearly laid out for me, but it zigzagged more than I had ever expected. I made some wrong turns and faced obstacles that felt like dead ends. I had to find my way forward and stumbled by taking it all on my shoulders. When faced with difficult feedback, I reflected inward critically, viewed my situation as a catastrophe, and almost severed one of the most important relationships of my career. Once I paused and eventually learned more, I could open the mirrored door to find an exit from the maze.

I know now from the hundreds of women I've worked with, the research I've done, and my own experience that women face many barriers, both internal and external, that are different from men's challenges. These obstacles frequently stem from our culturally conditioned perspectives and resulting embedded habits. Women struggle to gain credibility in a culture that is ambivalent about seeing them in leadership roles. They sense something is off but get limited clarity and little direct, honest communication. This puts us squarely in front of our own mirrored door, trying to fix ourselves and our situation to step into a leadership identity. We must recognize, though, that past conditioning and resulting habits are systemic. We navigate work as though it were a mirrored maze. We struggle, reflect inward when we face a wall, look for light to show us the right path, and find our way through trial and error.

Walking the Tightrope

I realize now that the feedback I received was a result of senior management's perceptions of what a leader looks like. Although I would have benefited from speaking up more, the question of my toughness was rooted in one of the most common challenges women face in the workplace today: the double bind that occurs when women are held to embedded biases about their gender while also being measured against standards of leadership linked to masculinity.

To be fair, biases and embedded expectations are a part of human nature; they are cognitive shortcuts. They can help us be more efficient (walk the faster block) or protect ourselves (I shouldn't walk through that dark alley). But they become a problem when they are unconscious and limit our own or others' opportunities. While conscious discrimination and stereotyping were much more blatant and prevalent in the 1970s to '90s, and therefore easier to see, Herminia Ibarra's research indicates that a second-generation bias continues in more hidden ways. She likens it to "something in the water" that impacts women's opportunities as opposed to the blatant discrimination in the past.

The double bind for women is driven by both expectations of leadership and gender. If I asked you to describe a leader, you'd likely use words like "assertive," "self-confident," "task-driven," "commanding," "independent," and "self-promoting." The characteristics come from a more hierarchical definition of leadership, when organizational culture almost entirely comprised top-down, command-and-control environments. While the average workplace has since become more collaborative, our past expectations of leaders are still in our subconscious. And these traits are much more typically associated with masculinity.

If I asked you to describe women, you'd likely choose words like "helpful," "sympathetic," "nurturing," "relationship-focused," and "advocate for others." Researchers refer to these traits as communal, another way of saying "other"-oriented. While women can be leaders and exhibit leadership traits, our first reaction is to assess them relative to our instinctive view of their gender, not of leadership. And usually, something doesn't seem quite right. If they fit the preconceived notions of women, their traits don't match up with what is expected of a leader. And if they fit the bill for a leader, then they don't come across as feminine and, therefore, are less likeable.

This dynamic creates a catch-22. Women have a perceived trade-off—should I act more the way people expect of me as a woman or as a leader? This is a "damned if you do, doomed if you don't" position. Women walk the tightrope of expectations as they manage others' perceptions and face the quick judgment of being too soft or too hard, never just right.

Catalyst's research found that both men *and* women grant and assume more competence to men as leaders because of our long-held images of what a workplace leader looks like. Our society expects women to be focused on others, not themselves, making it more difficult for women to self-advocate—and creating a more negative impression when they do. We've trained women to negotiate for themselves, yet they continually face a greater risk of backlash when they do. We expect women to be warm, friendly, and non-confrontational, and penalties for behaving outside that expectation can be high. This likeability-competence gap sets up a dynamic where women expend significant energy navigating this gap—time that could be better spent elsewhere. When women show more ambition and dominance, people may perceive them as more arrogant, ruthless, and bossy though the same actions are considered leaderlike in men. So women strategize about how to show leadership while being gender consistent in a world that views those traits as contrary.

Walking this tightrope of expectations probably feels familiar and frustrating. I tell my students in my Women's Leadership Seminar series that my job is to help them navigate the world that is, so they can go create the one they all wish they had.

I'm grateful Chuck risked telling me about senior leadership questioning my toughness. It motivated me to speak up with stronger opinions and to share my business plans in a more decisive way. I rethought how I approached each new audience. With sales, my goal was to motivate salespeople to deliver the revenue. With the CEO and his team, I was building their confidence that our profit plan was solid—going after new opportunities to create upside, with contingencies in place should something unexpected happen. My boss coached me to show the kind of leadership that mattered in the boardroom while encouraging me to be myself. I didn't really change. I turned up the volume on my thinking and planning, which was harder to see in those high-pressure, less-frequent venues with the top brass.

"Know the Book on You"

One of the best ways to deal with this double bind is to reflect on your style and get feedback from those around you. In my Personal Leadership Insights course, I ask MBA students to seek feedback from three people in their careers or lives who are "loving critics," a term that author and psychologist Tasha Eurich uses to describe people who care about you and your future enough to give you the straight scoop. Chuck was reluctant to do that for me at first; but without that knowledge, I don't know that I would have ever stepped up to show my ownership and accountability. As I took little steps of courage with my opinions, I became more confident and took more risks. I encourage you to find ways to "know the book on you." By that I mean understand what is said about you when you aren't in the room. Know your results and reputation, along with what others recall of interactions with you. When those who decide your career have a limited window on your work, they may count on the perspectives of others or trust their own conclusions, even with limited exposure to you.

Research indicates that women receive less actionable and vaguer feedback. Neither men nor women want to hurt feelings, be seen as a bad person, or trigger an emotional reaction of tears or anger. In today's post–#MeToo world, some may see giving feedback as more treacherous than before. While most men are not worried about accusations of harassment or criminal behavior, they are more afraid than they once were of saying something wrong or unintentionally discriminatory. A 2021 study in the *Personality and Social Psychology Bulletin* indicated that women were given inflated performance feedback compared to men. In receiving well-intended but less accurate feedback, or "little white lies," women may be unaware of their blind spots and development opportunties. This means we need to strengthen our ability to give, get, and gain from feedback to navigate the tightrope of expectations and the possible reluctance of managers. My advice in this area is the following.

Give permission for feedback. Let the key people you work with know how valuable their input will be for your development. Set the stage at transitions so you communicate to others how you want to work, and set up a give-and-take of feedback after project milestones or during your one-on-one meetings. When you demonstrate your openness to other's ideas, you may

Women strategize about how to show leadership while being gender consistent in a world that views those traits as contrary.

help them become more open to your input. Be ready to give helpful, actionable, timely opinions on how you can improve.

Create a list of powerful questions. Use these at the start of a role or relationship. When I enter a new job, I meet with my key stakeholders and ask a set of questions to learn more about them and their expectations and concerns. Two of my favorites are "What do you hope I will do?" and "What do you fear I'll do?" I've found these questions more helpful than any set of performance objectives because they help someone identify what success looks like and what worries might be on their mind. I also love Marshall Goldsmith's "feedforward" concept to provide questions about the future—for example, "What's one thing I can do better the next time I manage a product launch?" This approach keeps things focused on the future and makes it easier for the giver to come up with something specific you can act on. Imagine if I had calmly asked Chuck, "What would 'being tough enough' look like in those quarterly meetings?"

Take in feedback with curiosity. When we have succeeded, we expect more of the same. When negative comments or results come our way, we have less practice dealing with them. Our emotions can flare up, like mine did, and we may get defensive. A mirrored door drops down in front of us, and we personalize it and disrupt the learning conversation. But when we look through a lens of curiosity, we open ourselves to growth and can see new ideas and more possibility. And most importantly, we don't shoulder all the blame for negative feedback and perceptions of us: others' systems and biases are part of the feedback we receive. Get curious about the processes, systems, and culture and how they contribute to the issue. Curiosity gives us distance and objectivity. What if I had gotten curious about the toughness required of leadership? What if Chuck had gotten curious about why I was so quiet in those quarterly meetings?

Decide what feedback you will act on. Although I became a more effective communicator because of the feedback from Chuck, there was a time when acting on certain feedback would not have honored who I am. The point is to know who you are, where you stand, and what you want, so you can determine how you want to participate. This can also help you clarify the kind of culture that enables you to thrive, so you can find a place that fits.

Remember that feedback is more about the giver and the way they view the world. In my case, the senior executives saw my warmth and likeability but not my decisions, plans, and ability to lead others and make the tough calls. I was fortunate to have Chuck coach me to find that balance. I now see my tendencies and how I can be perceived. I've worked hard and have learned to show the rest of me, but still fall back into past patterns. "Knowing the book on you" can be invaluable in taking the lead, telling the story you want to tell, and opening the mirrored door.

Mirror, Mirror in the Maze, How Will I Ever Get My Raise?

Eventually, I cooled off and talked to Chuck openly about my disappointments and hopes. It was helpful to acknowledge what I felt was going on, and he joined me in discussing the elephant of perception sitting in the room. Together we developed ways for me to become more visible. I hated the word "showcase," but I suppose that is what I did. I always believed perception was reality. As a result, I got to work.

I continued to be coached by Chuck and mentored by my circle. I reached out to other leaders to get to know them, build rapport, seek advice, and share my career goals. I realized that my network was deep but small and narrow. I joined a company-wide recruitment committee that expanded my connections across divisions and broadened my perspective into innovations and challenges happening elsewhere.

I learned how the communication style I, like many women, had learned in childhood (to downplay our talent and achievements) made me less comfortable taking credit or sharing victories. It inadvertently robbed me of holding my own with the senior team.

I previously struggled with the notion of self-promotion as bragging and inauthentic. Over time, I learned to confidently share what I was working on or had achieved. I'm not going to lie: at first it was hard and felt a bit slimy. I always looked down on the guys who talked a good game, assigning some of them big egos and empty suits. Chuck showed me otherwise. He was an amazing role model as he exhibited humility, grace, and ease while confidently sharing his successes and failures, something I aspired to convey. He became an advocate for inclusive leadership and modeled the way for many.

Over time, I knew I answered the question of toughness when the CEO scheduled time with me one-on-one to discuss my future. The prior month, I had recommended restructuring one of my businesses, including shutting down a facility that had excess manufacturing capacity. It was the right thing to do for the business and market, and I was glad to gain the support and alignment from above. Immediately following the plan presentation, Chuck came to my cube to congratulate me on how well it went and found me in tears. My heart broke for the people who would be impacted and likely laid off or transferred by the closing of that small plant. I wondered if I had the strength to make these tough calls after all.

When I met with the CEO weeks later, he told me how impressed he was that I could be smart and decisive about the business and such an advocate for the people evidenced by how hard I fought to support their transition into new roles. He told me that balance makes the best leader, but it is all too rare. I was thrilled to finally be seen and, like Chuck, have tried ever since to show that it can be done.

I always wanted to be a leader but wondered how I'd be able to do some of the hard things needed for the sake of the business results. I found the answer in those "other"-oriented traits, like empathy and sensitivity, which helped me connect the needs of our people *and* the enterprise. It helped me handle difficult people issues with care, compassion, and dignity. By doing so, I was able to develop a tender power melded from who I was and what I had grown to be.

I eventually became a vice president, thanks to amazing coaching and advocacy together with my own focus on presence, point of view, and progress. With the foundation of what I learned, I successfully navigated my trajectory through multiple industries. Chuck and other mentors helped me see myself as more than what I could have imagined. I eventually held the top brand post in divisions of multiple industries, became a board director, and led a consulting firm as president.

When Korn Ferry Institute interviewed fifty-seven female CEOs at Fortune 1000 companies, 65 percent of the women reported that they didn't know they were CEO material until someone told them they could do it and recognized their talent. Whether or not you aspire to be a CEO, there is power in imagining a bigger possibility for yourself that you may not have recognized could happen. You can likely do more than you realize. If you are managing others, you can change their lives by believing in and building their vision of their future.

Chuck passed away from cancer in 2019. When we celebrated his life, we recalled a Gatorade advertisement he had co-developed, called "Be Like Mike," starring Michael Jordan. As we toasted to our leader's life, we all received T-shirts with one of the most important lessons: "Be Like Chuck." When faced with a tough business, people, or career decision, I still think, "What would Chuck do?"

The Reality of the Workload

We face dramatic shifts with women's rising level of education and career ambitions, delayed and declining marriage rates, and economic needs for single- or dual-career incomes amid rising costs. While technology allows us to work from anywhere, it also contributes to the creation of "greedy work," a term coined by professor and author Claudia Goldin. She traces the transition from the forty-hour workweek to the sixty-to-eighty-hour workweek in consulting, investment banking, and tech. Immediate responses and availability on nights and weekends have become the norm. And the rewards for this 24/7 kind of commitment are extremely attractive, even while we know up front about the staggering risks to our relationships, well-being, and experience of a personal life. Goldin connects the rise of greedy jobs to pay inequity for women as she cites the inability for dual-career couples to sustain the exhausting workplace expectations of the sixty-to-eighty-hour workweek in some professions. Is it any wonder that COVID prompted so many to rethink their careers and lives?

Today's employees want a more collaborative, humanistic culture at work. When we make changes that improve the possibilities for women, we are likely making it better for everyone. Many men don't want the past role played by their fathers, of being the sole breadwinner who has little time with their kids. They want a new way of working too.

When it began in 2021, the Great Resignation seemed initially to focus on job changes and exits from one maze to another. As more people, especially women, left organizations in greater numbers to rethink careers or create their own businesses, a new theme emerged. Maybe the Resignation is less "take this job and shove it" and more "take this work and change it." Perhaps the post-traumatic growth from the pandemic will result in a workplace that is less a maze and more a raise, where standards, pay, and humanity are heightened for all. Smart companies know this and are scrambling to offer what they think will attract great talent. Perhaps the smartest thing they can do is hire, develop, and reward leaders who can truly take care *and* take charge, merging the talents of all genders and demographics to create the leadership needs of the future. In that future and in those places, women are well equipped to lead the way, thrive, and transform.

Men in the Mirror

"I can't believe they're asking this of us. My wife and kids are going to kill me," said Brad, our head of sales, after muting the call so the other city couldn't hear our comments.

"This is unbelievable," Mike, our ops lead, chimed in next, shaking his head. "Is this how it's going to be in this company?"

"It is what it is," grumbled Brad.

"How are you going to tell your family?" Mike asked.

Our company had been acquired by a large multinational corporation. Overnight, our division was now reporting in to a business unit in another city, leaving the three of us as the leadership team in Chicago. Like many people facing major organizational changes such as this, we were navigating how to handle working with the mothership.

The three of us huddled in a conference room as we learned the next steps to finalizing our new strategic plan, which included a trip to headquarters the following week. When the

VP of strategy told us we needed to meet for breakfast before the 7:30 meeting on November 1, I looked at my calendar and showed the guys that this meant flying out the night before, which was Halloween. We each had little kids primed for the most fun night of the fall, and they were in those precious few years where they still gladly trick-or-treated with their parents. The guys' frowns told me they thought the date and time were a done deal, that the sacrifice came with the territory of work and leadership.

I unclicked the mute button and said, "I have a conflict the evening before, but I will take the earliest morning flight." Brad's and Mike's expressions changed as we awaited the response.

"That will be fine, just let me know your timing. We'll just start when you get here."

Seeing an opportunity, Mike added, "I'll just fly out when Ellen does."

"Me too," Brad chimed in, and we all waited for the reaction.

"That works," was barely uttered. Mike and Brad silently raised their arms in touchdown formation.

At the time, I felt I was taking one for the team and rolled my eyes at them, then laughed. Now I look back and think that my male colleagues wanted what I did but didn't have the organizational safety to say they were prioritizing family over work. They faced a different set of risks to show they were company men and uphold the "strongman" image. While it wasn't exactly safe for me to say what I did, it was easier and safer in some ways. Fortunately, I found becoming a mom enabled me to draw boundaries more than I had been able to in the past.

While that was decades ago, and shared parenting responsibilities and work travel have evolved, the story is emblematic of what I hear from my male clients, colleagues, and students. Men are held to expectations too. They are adapting and learning and may also feel like strangers as the ground under them shifts. Though the workplace was built for the guys, it didn't equip them to know how to handle their own changing interests and identities in a workplace built for a different time.

With a better-late-than-never increased awareness of the challenges women face at work, many men, even the best ones, struggle to know what to do and worry about saying or doing the wrong thing. I don't mean criminal actions; I mean something that could unknowingly offend or mark them as sexist. And many times, in their worry, they avoid risks and do nothing at all.

I believe the majority of men want to help women and improve the workplace, but they face their own ingrained expectations that seem to require them to be strong, man up, and avoid emotions so as not to lower their perceived status.

We are all on a journey but face different obstacles. Being raised in a family that believed in me and being taught by many leaders who helped me navigate my way truly gave me a leg up and hastened my travels. If you find yourself a bit lost, it's easy to turn inward with doubt or outward with blame. My suggestion is to remember it is not your fault, and more than likely it is not the fault of your current colleagues, who may also be finding their way through the maze. We can drive change when we match company values to actions that include what is rewarded and penalized. We can bring the softer skills of collaboration and care to the traditional command-and-control behaviors to attract and retain the best of today's workforce. As Gandhi said, "The change begins with me."

KEY TAKEAWAYS

- When the workplace triggers consistent doubt and hesitation, it can feel like a mirrored maze, where we constantly question ourselves at each mirrored door.

- We need to share our goals and aspirations so our bosses do not assume we lack ambition.

- Senior leaders, who can influence our careers, see only a small snapshot of who we are. Understanding how we are perceived is critical to knowing what we haven't yet seen about ourselves.

- Giving and getting feedback are important skills. When we permit others to give us feedback and ask powerful questions, we may gain valuable information about ourselves.

- Even if we don't fully identify with being a leader, we need to try on that identity and believe we have what it takes. True leaders use their hearts and minds to lead.

JOURNAL PROMPTS

- Choose three people you could ask for feedback and five open-ended questions that could help you "know the book on you." Here are some ideas: *What can you count on me for? How do I get in my own way? What are my blind spots? What is one thing I could do to elevate my standing with you and the senior team?*

- How might you share your career goals with your manager? What will show you that the decision makers know what you want for your career?

- What strengths do you bring to your team and company? What is your impact? How do those qualities define your leadership style?

4

The Inner Antagonist

*"I was once afraid of people saying,
'Who does she think she is?' Now I have the
courage to stand and say, 'This is who I am.'"*
OPRAH WINFREY

"F@#K! F@#K! F@#K!"

"What's wrong?" my husband yelled as he bolted into my home office assuming a large object had fallen on me. If you knew me, you would know that I rarely say, much less scream, curse words unless I'm about to have a car crash.

"What was I thinking? Why did I apply, and why did I say yes?" I muttered. "I just got off a call with the TEDx organizer. Believe it or not, they want me to do a talk."

"That's so cool! You've always wanted to do this. Congratulations!" Ned exclaimed with a huge smile on his face. Then he noticed my expression. "I don't get it, what's wrong?"

"I don't have enough time. I have to go to a rehearsal in a few weeks. There is no way. I'm not ready. I'm a backup option anyway," I replied. "But I just agreed. *Gaah!*"

"But you just did that keynote. Can't you use that?" he said. "This is really exciting!"

"Not for me," I said, frustrated. "Don't you get it? I'm stuck here. Why did I say yes? That keynote is forty-five minutes, and this talk is fifteen minutes. It's harder to write something shorter. They need a summary of my big idea by next week. It's all been said before."

"You always say you won't do well and then you do fine," Ned reminded me. "You always pull it off, Ellen."

"Not this time. TED is different. I could make a fool of myself on video, and it will be online forever!" I said, imagining an epic viral form of embarrassment lurking underneath this commitment.

"I thought this was on your bucket list. It's such an opportunity. Can I do anything to help you get ready?"

"Yes, call them back and cancel," I said with a smile at my mix of emotions. "No, you're right. I do want this. I've always wanted this. Let me figure out how to make it happen."

The questions that circled my mind hurled me back to a group meeting six months earlier when a colleague gave me feedback that summed up how I had been showing up in my newish job. I was part of a teaching team piloting a new exercise for our course during which we acknowledged each other for three to five minutes. We also shared a wish for each other's future or to achieve something we were working on, or a hope for each of us to get out of our own way. After receiving some wonderful words describing me like "accomplished, tender-hearted, and courageous," I steadied myself for the area of improvement.

"My wish for you is that you stop hiding your light under a bushel," said Professor Shana Carroll, a fellow teacher in the leadership development group.

While my Catholic school upbringing left me unsure of the specific Bible verses, I knew every word to *Godspell*, a '70s musical about Jesus and his apostles set in modern times. In a flash, I recalled the lyrics to "Light of the World" and knew what she meant. I had a lot more to give and share but was holding back. Shana had been instrumental in hiring me for my first role at Kellogg and knew me well. She was my go-to source of knowledge on transitioning to academia. She had this insightful ability to observe what was happening, tie together different conversations, and tell people what they needed to hear.

When I arrived at the school, another colleague had given me some friendly advice to not overplay my extensive corporate career.

"That won't sit well with the tenured professors that consider themselves the 'real professors,'" they said with air quotes. "Never ever say things like 'in the real world' as opposed to their theoretical world of case studies and research. Clinicals were hired to complement their 'brilliance,'" they added again with the air quotes. "With high bid points and teaching ratings, we do pretty well."

As a newbie, I quickly understood the pecking order and the reason for the frequency of my colleague's air quotes. To succeed, I had to watch myself. I didn't want to get sideways with any tenured professors, especially when I was securing their participation to teach in my Women's Leadership Program. I was in awe of the expertise, presence, and confidence of the female professors I worked with on my seminar series. They knew how to command a room with their academic knowledge, MBA courses, and engaging stories from their consulting clients or companies in which they had taught.

While I learned so much from them and from auditing courses, their greatness made me feel small. I marveled at their extensive expertise in their given fields and thought I could never come close to that. They asked for what they wanted and commanded respect, while I was on guard to remember my place. I had to learn how to understand and teach MBA students who were decades younger than me. My switch to the academic world was hard. I wasn't used to being a beginner again and didn't like being on a steep learning curve after years of being the one who knew her stuff.

During our team exercise, post-acknowledgments, everyone seemed to glow and expressed appreciation for what was shared. I took in Shana's comments and felt seen in her words and the nuance of her language. No one had ever quite described me the way she did, and I cherished it. But that was short-lived. True to form, I focused on one aspect of her wish—the way in which I held back.

I felt somewhat encouraged but primarily stung. Though we teach our MBA students that feedback is a gift, I was not feeling grateful. The group's approval mattered to me, especially because I was new. Shana's comment signaled to me that I wasn't where I or she wanted me to be. At the same time, she reinforced that I had so much to share, and she wanted me to say more, show more, and be more. I wondered if I was guilty of the same thing that disappointed me when my female students didn't raise their hands.

As I reflected on her comments, I recalled different opportunities in my first year that I could have jumped on. I had been asked to do a talk about overcoming doubt, called "Hear My Story," for a student club and declined. I had been asked to do a speech about my career for a large gathering and was conveniently out of town. I was asked to comment on a #MeToo story in a major publication and didn't reply in time. I was scared to risk the reveal when all around me I saw male C-suite veterans teaching students through their real-world experience. I was one of the few female professors who had climbed the corporate ladder to great heights, with so many stories to tell, and I was falling down on the job. Worse yet, the class I was learning to teach was built on the premise that the most self-aware and vulnerable leaders are the ones who create the greatest connections with their people as they model knowing and showing themselves.

Shana was right. I was dimming my light and playing small. I was afraid.

Her words weighed on me. In the past I would have disregarded the praise and stayed in the disappointment of the constructive feedback. But once I had reflected on all my missed opportunities to step into the professorial role, her comments became a call to be my best. She believed in me, and that opened me up to see the kindness in giving candid, direct feedback. That session and her caring, straightforward message became a catalyst. I recognized that I had gotten my dream job teaching at my alma mater after an accomplished career but was psyching myself out because I was triggered by the challenges of my career pivot. My long list of disempowering messages that continually popped into my head must have shown on the outside.

Back then, I would add up the reasons why I wasn't a legitimate professor or couldn't be a women's leadership expert. I had a notion that I needed to be humble and respect the expertise and experience that surrounded me. To explain my shortcomings to myself and sometimes out loud I made deflective statements like, "I'm new to teaching," "I'm not really an academic," or "I'm from marketing, not HR." In lower moments, I ruminated and wondered, *Who am I to talk about my experiences? Will students really be interested in my story? Am I really ready and prepared to do this?* I stacked all my doubts to form a protective wall I couldn't see past. Shana's words were like a pickax that broke open a hole in my careful construction. In a moment, new light streamed in, and the wall began to crack.

Once reality set in that it was time to hang up this coat of doubt, I decided to act. I attended storytelling speaker training, which gave me more practice and a wider range of choices in content and presentations. I took more risks with my class, Personal Leadership Insights, and finally got more personal in my stories. As I shared the good, the bad, and the ugly of my twenty-five-year corporate career, I found greater engagement, appreciation, and ratings from my students. Surprisingly, telling on myself helped my students do the same and taught them

that vulnerability does not equal weakness. My doubts still sur-
faced but with less frequency and stickiness. My small steps
propelled bigger ones and my comfort grew.

And then one day, I read that my Chicago suburb was planning to launch an inaugural TEDxWomen event. On a lark, I
applied, thinking, *Why not?*

Almost immediately, Heather Hehman, the program founder
and organizer, emailed my rejection with warmth and support.

Thank God! I thought with relief as I learned that the speakers
had already been chosen. I was glad to put it out of my mind and
replied graciously with good wishes and a promise to attend later
that year. Two months later, Heather called me out of the blue.

"We've found that we want to balance our group of speakers
and their backgrounds. We think you'd be a great fit, as you
bring an academic perspective. Are you willing to reapply and
be ready in the shorter time frame?" Heather asked.

"Yes!" I uttered in an instant without looking at my calendar.
"But you do know I'm a clinical professor, not tenured, right?" I
asked, wondering if I belonged on their stage, since they were
looking for *a real academic.*

"We want you if you can be ready. We really like your message," she confirmed, and wrapped up the call with detailed
next steps of the aggressive schedule.

At first, I was thrilled. Then the timeline hit me. Then the
visibility. Then the F-bombs.

My husband's excitement over the news was thrilling. At the
same time, I was terrified by what I had committed to. The realization that I would be on video for all the world to see made
my anxiety skyrocket.

Shana's comments led me to make meaningful changes
over time, but in that moment, I viewed Shana as the culprit of
my current bind. Picturing her, I thought, *Now look what you
made me do.*

The Voice of Judgment

We so frequently worry about what others think of us, but our toughest critic is usually the one in our heads. It usually speaks in a harsher or more hostile voice than we would ever use with someone else in our life. I call this voice the Inner Antagonist. You may remember from high school English literature class that the antagonist is the one who opposes, or the adversary. In physiological terms, antagonism is a muscle that contracts and limits the movement of the muscle that it is paired with as it reduces physiological activity. The Inner Antagonist is that opposing, harsh voice that restricts actions. To be sure, I am all for the consideration of pros, cons, and risks before acting. But sometimes we are overwhelmed in that assessment by the adversarial voice, and we limit our own momentum.

When our internal messages speak in judgment, they antagonize our presence and our progress with a layer of anxiety and stress. The Inner Antagonist is cunning, as it checks all the boxes to ensure we get stuck in front of the mirrored door. We hesitate at opportunity, feel unready to take risk, and wait for certainty. This clouds our thinking and decision-making. We spend our time preparing so that we can eventually open the mirrored door. This familiar feeling fools us into thinking we are safe. The risk is that by the time we finally feel ready, the opportunity may have already passed.

When opportunity knocks, we must open the door. In my new job, I opened the door but immediately slammed it shut again. I cracked it ajar, but the voice in my head put the chain on while opportunity was waiting for me. My commitment to do the TEDx talk forced me to pass over the threshold but not without a lot of sleepless nights, stress, and hesitancy. I was so busy perfecting, pleasing, preparing, and posing to fit in that I was not moving forward and showing myself.

I saw this inner adversary or antagonist not only in myself, but also in my students, clients, former colleagues, and friends in so many areas of our lives, regardless of the stakes. I was surprised by how common hesitancy was in advanced-degree students. An article in the *Harvard Gazette* in 2011 perfectly captured the reluctant thought process during the internal classroom participation debate in our heads.

"There's a fake-out in the beginning where my trigger hand jumps up to answer a question from the professor, only to pretend to caress a stray hair and tuck it securely behind my ear," Susan Cheng wrote. "Then there's the psych-out move. Ideas flow, but they're not perfect yet, nor do I have quite the right formulation of words. I don't want to make a fool of myself. Time passes and I know I need to get into the discussion but can't manage to raise my hand. Finally, there's the strikeout, where just as my hand is about to spring up, someone else makes my point, and the discussion careens forward in a different way. Class ends. Another missed opportunity."

How often do we fake, psych, or strike out when opportunities arrive? Cheng's comical narrative described what I was seeing: stages of reluctance and half-hearted participation, declared shortcomings, delayed readiness, then disappointment. It made me wonder how often we snooze and lose on our way to the perfect comment, proposal, or crowd-pleasing idea outside the classroom. Women told me about avoiding registration for the harder classes, their strategies to avoid being unexpectedly called on in class, and their stress at networking events. These observations helped me recognize this same avoidance in myself and find the courage to bring it out into the open.

The Imposter Awakens

I was struck by the emails full of self-doubt from so many people with so many accomplishments. Like the brilliant MBA students who didn't raise their hands in orientation, we over-think the risk of others' views and undervalue our own much needed contribution. I kept hearing women share a sense that they were not up to a certain situation and would be exposed despite credentials and a track record of success. These leaders offhandedly referred to themselves as having "imposter syndrome," a concept first theorized and researched by Pauline Clance and Suzanne Imes in 1978 as "impostor phenomenon." The researchers described imposter syndrome as the persistent belief of mainly high-achieving women that they are not actually bright and are fooling anyone who thinks they are. The tie to gender was meaningful at the time because the study was done when women were initially entering the workplace in greater numbers. Clance and Imes found that early family dynamics and gender stereotyping contributed to the development of imposter syndrome in women. Their clinical experience indicates that women face it with greater frequency and more intensity than men.

When we secretly believe we are an imposter, the risk of being found out elevates our fear. We think we are the only one who feels this way and therefore want to hide it. We suffer in silence as we overcompensate with more work, risk avoidance, and posed confidence. The reality is that we are not alone. In her book *The Secret Thoughts of Successful Women*, Valerie Young states that an overwhelming 70 percent of high achievers have imposter syndrome. It's as if we believe our past achievements don't count, as though we are always starting from scratch instead of building on what we can bring to a role.

Young highlights three triggers of imposter doubts: transitions, tenure, and expertise. I see this play out with my students, clients, colleagues, and myself.

First, transitions are a critical part of our development but make us ripe for doubt. Whether because of earning an educational degree, a new job or company, or a promotion, our minds can overthink our qualifications, our fit with those around us, and our likelihood of success. I see these doubts flare up in the MBA courses I teach, during first-semester midterms, which are unfortunately timed with the start of the recruitment season. The business school honeymoon is over, and students are convinced they will do badly on their exams and never get the internship they desire. At its best, imposter syndrome is motivation to buckle down and study and prepare for interviews. At its worst, some students catastrophize their outlook in the short term. Getting that first term under their belts gives students the knowledge they can do it.

Second, tenure in a role, profession, or industry can bring on imposter syndrome too. It's counterintuitive because longer tenure means greater knowledge and, we assume, a higher level of confidence. But the imposter feelings are rooted in imagining that others expect we know everything. One of my former clients compared her industry knowledge of three years to her boss's command of the details from his twenty years in the business. She found herself reading industry books on the weekends, lying in wait for a question she could not answer.

"If I can't answer their questions, then everyone will know I'm not as a good as my boss. How can they see me as his heir apparent when I should know what he knows?" she confided in me. The reality was that the C-suite leaders knew she hadn't lived through the history of the industry, and they advocated for her anyway.

Lastly, expertise can trigger imposter syndrome and heighten one's sense of risk especially in certain fields. In industries

When our internal messages speak in judgment, they antagonize our presence and our progress with a layer of anxiety and stress.

with rapid change or technological advancements, there is so much more to keep updated on and learn. This can increase individual doubts for those in medical, legal, or technology firms, to name a few.

"Even though we've done everything that experts advise and have never had a breach, I can't shake the feeling that I've missed something," a chief information security officer told me. The reality is that the pace of change is exponential, yet leaders expect of themselves that they must be able to keep up. The high risks of a negative outcome in these fields reinforce this expectation of self. When faced with this tall order, is it any wonder their imposter feelings are triggered?

But the silence is breaking as courageous people share their thoughts of doubt. Michelle Obama wrote about her imposter feelings in her book *Becoming*. She is a powerful example of normalizing our inner doubts that, regardless of what we've done to date, we don't belong at the next level of success. When we get stuck in past messages and conditioned habits, we stay in place and miss the growth on the other side of the mirrored door. At times, we get in our own way, but women also face many systemic barriers to bigger opportunities.

When people have been marginalized, because of biases toward their gender, race, sexual orientation, ability, income, and so on, the imposter in them may rear its ugly head more easily and swiftly. This can also be true of first-timers, such as first-generation college students, people with uncommon backgrounds in homogenous cultures, or state college graduates in Ivy League MBA education.

When a part of our identity has been stereotyped in the past, we can quickly assess a situation, a room, or an organization to assume how others might view us and how we may or may not fit. When we belong, we feel safer, more at ease, and likely more confident. The fewer people who look and sound like us, the more our self-belief can be challenged. Combating this can suck up a lot of energy, as can microaggressions or biased slights that all too often further antagonize us.

In one of the most often downloaded articles from the *Harvard Business Review*, "Stop Telling Women They Have Imposter Syndrome," Ruchika Tulshyan and Jodi-Ann Burey question why we put the onus of imposter syndrome on women's shoulders. They point out that the number one job is to fix the systemic biases in our organizations instead of focusing on fixing women. Their follow-up, "End Imposter Syndrome in Your Workplace," outlines steps organizations need to take to diversify what leadership looks and acts like when disrupting our conditioned expectations. While I believe many women and men genuinely feel like imposters and can work to reframe their belonging in their roles, I applaud and encourage the focus on how companies and leaders can more aggressively disrupt the current old-school leadership model and workplace culture.

When we let the voice of the Inner Antagonist, in the form of imposter syndrome, overtake our shot at growth, we lose, and so do our organizations. We must recognize it and mark it as a sign that we are expanding our skills, experiences, and possibilities as individuals, and building more creativity, stronger problem solving, and smarter risk-taking into our companies.

Gender Stereotypes Impact Women's Confidence

Recent research shows that gender stereotypes influence women's beliefs in their own abilities, as mentioned in chapter 1. Katherine B. Coffman's studies indicate that these self-beliefs shape decisions about our career choices, willingness to share ideas, and interest in seeking a promotion. When we buy into these stereotypes, we see a distorted, negative self-image.

"Women are more likely than men to shrug off the praise and lowball their own abilities," Coffman discovered. She found women fall prey to feeling less confident than men in certain subjects, like math, that were stereotypically presumed to be a strength for men. In the research, even in experiments where women performed similarly, they guessed their results were worse and had a hard time believing they were comparably talented. Coffman's studies also indicated that women held back their ideas in topics that were considered more male domains of expertise.

While Coffman and her colleagues continue to work on interventions to close the confidence gap, she advises leaders to consider how this issue impacts work and processes. Breaking down these biases in your organization, providing extra feedback with evidence, adding processes that allow for everyone's input and ideas, and highlighting career possibilities are a great place to begin.

For individuals, consider how stereotypes might be warping your self-view or leading you to withhold your contribution or candidacy. Are your inner thoughts always from an antagonistic point of view? Maybe they urge you on or perhaps they drag you down? What would it take to balance the Inner Antagonist with an Inner Protagonist? What would work and life be like if the question in your mind became, "Why not me?"

I am on a mission to accelerate others' journeys through a simple framework I call ACT. It has helped me, and I use it with my coaching clients and students to tackle the doubtful messages so we can have more ease, comfort, and self-care. It's simple and easy to understand, and you can start immediately by committing to three steps.

1. **Assess the critique and validity.** This requires an awareness of your inner dialogue around doubts, imposter syndrome, and self-belief, and how you respond. Consider:

- What facts or feedback do you have, or could you get, to build your objectivity? What is the tone, message, and underlying belief of your inner voice? Is it harsh or fair?

- What's your MO in response to the voice? How does that benefit you? Is there a price you pay?

My Inner Antagonist seeded questions like, "Who am I to give a TED talk?" When I assessed my inner dialogue, it was as if I stayed in that question and churned in the implied unworthiness for this honor. When I realized I was doing this, I shifted my thinking to an answer, which was about my experience climbing the corporate ladder and growing expertise on advancing women. It helped me quiet the voice and spend my energy building myself up rather than questioning my merits.

2. Channel your Inner Protagonist. Do this to counterbalance and quiet the Inner Antagonist. You want to hear more from this voice and increase its frequency and intensity.

- How would you talk to others facing doubts (in words and tone), and how can you bring that compassion to yourself?

- When you've been encouraged, seen, and guided positively, what was the tone and message of the voice?

- What would you be like if you let up on perfecting, pleasing, preparing endlessly, pushing, and posing? What would it take to be ready enough?

- What message do you long to hear and want to believe? What is a shorthand way to recall that feeling in challenging moments?

I channeled my energy into self-compassion. I now thought having these fears before a talk like this was simply being human. Doing this helped me get realistic about my concerns, which were less about my credentials and more about the content of the talk and my comfort with public speaking. This clarity focused my thinking and next steps.

3. Tackle the next best step toward your goals. Thinking, reframing, and channeling will help but are insufficient unless you act. When you shift your behaviors, you shift your thinking. This is about putting yourself in motion.

- What are you trying to accomplish?

- What is one small action that could help your momentum?

- How might you summon your courage to act before you feel 100 percent certainty?

I tackled my practice plan, which kicked me into action. Once I was taking tangible steps to improve my talk and comfort level, the critical voice grew distant and lost its hold on me. I learned that where I focus my mind and energy made a world of difference, and that I can use this knowledge next time the Inner Antagonist pipes up.

Ideas Worth Sharing

What was I thinking? screamed the voice in my head.

Backstage on the big day, I was a bundle of nerves. The audience in the auditorium was abuzz with excitement as I tried to tune out my fellow speakers who were practicing their speeches aloud. The high school student assigned to help me kept telling me she could never do a TEDx talk. Her innocent truth reflected everything I had been saying to myself and fueled me to see if I could change her mind with my talk. I told myself that even if only one person was inspired to "take center stage of her life," then my talk would be worth it.

When I was called to be on deck and ready at the stage entrance, I tried to calm the trembling in my knees. As the stage manager checked my mic, she saw that a wire that snaked through my waistline up to my headpiece was bunched up.

"Let me redo this," she said. "How much tape did they use?"

"Thirty seconds," a stage volunteer called out.

"It's not working, and I don't want to hurt you or pull your hair," the stage manager whispered.

The MC began to introduce me.

"I don't care, just do it so I can get this done," I told her. She tore the tape off my hair as though ripping a bandage off my nerves—fast, painful, and much better afterward. It was the best last-minute distraction I could have asked for. It quelled my overthinking and propelled me into action.

"You did it!" said my daughter Katie, proudly, when I joined her post-talk in the lobby. After everything I had gone through to pull this off, I was so thrilled to see her face and know that she saw her mom do something that was scary, risky, and life-changing as a result. It wasn't perfect. There are moments I still cringe about when thinking about them, but I've never been prouder of myself for trying.

KEY TAKEAWAYS

- Our inner dialogue matters and can influence our mindset, actions, and well-being.

- Many women have an Inner Antagonist that hurts them when it is full of harsh judgments or convinces us to avoid all risk. It can prevent our growth and advancement.

- Imposter syndrome impacts 70 percent of high achievers. It may show up when we are stretching into a new situation, and especially where the norms and culture were not designed for us.

- We need to recognize how stereotypical beliefs can limit our risk-taking, and objectively consider and leverage our real capabilities and skills.

- Leaders must dismantle the ingrained, unfair views underlying the work culture, affirm women's talent and potential, and validate their value and voices.

JOURNAL PROMPTS

- Describe a time when you faced a new opportunity, fought the Inner Antagonist, and did something you are proud of.

- What got you through the challenge you describe above? Remind yourself of that next time the voice gets loud.

- Describe your Inner Antagonist's greatest hits. Which messages play on repeat? How might you reframe them using the ACT framework?

PART TWO

BREAK AWAY: RELEARNING SUCCESS STRATEGIES

In this part, I focus on five strategies that help women succeed but may also unintentionally sideline us. Each strategy can be both powerful *and*, at times, perilous, creating a double-edged sword. The following chapters highlight how the strategies work for us and against us, how they are linked to the mirrored door, and where we go from here. I've included managers' considerations to better coach individuals' progress, consider organizational obstacles, and spark courageous conversations.

The five strategies and potential perils of success are:

1 **Preparing to perfection.** This is the tendency to strive for the right answers, 100 percent certainty and accuracy, and always being the best.

2 **Eagerly pleasing.** This is prioritizing others and the greater good, listening collaboratively, building consensus, and keeping the peace.

3 **Fitting the mold.** This refers to the tendency to flex your agility to gain entry, fit in quickly, and follow the cultural norms to build familiarity and connection with the team.

4 **Working pedal to the metal.** This is the tendency to tirelessly drive for results, have a high capacity for work, and keep an eye on the prize.

5 **Performing patiently.** This describes proffering, the preference to deliver results, believe your work speaks for itself, understand your manager's timing and constraints, and be ready when it's your time.

When you build your awareness of each, you can lean into the upsides while mitigating the downsides. You may see yourself in one, a few, or all of them in different ways. I encourage you to be curious and consider what does or doesn't resonate, what underlying assumptions support your tendencies, and what, if anything, you want to evolve.

Preparing to Perfection

. . . .

"Have no fear of perfection; you'll never reach it."
ATTRIBUTED TO MARIE CURIE

"**DID EVERYTHING RIGHT...** I overdelivered on every project, role, and assignment they asked for or suggested. I've been working nonstop. But suddenly I feel like I've lost my luster in their eyes. I don't get it. What happened?" Elena, a director at a consumer products company, wondered aloud in our coaching session.

"Tell me more. What are you seeing that makes you feel this way?" I asked.

"I used to be the one whom my boss asked to handle things. I was the go-to who delivered perfect analysis. I was the confidante for where we were going next," she replied. "Now, I'm the last to know and never placed on the new initiative." Her voice broke.

"When did you begin to notice this?" I asked.

"I think it started to change when the team changed," Elena said. "When we were faced with that crisis last year, it was all hands on deck, and each director took parts of the plan. At the time, I felt proud of how we, and I, handled it. Then something started to change. I remember my manager asking me to make a call with the information we had. There was clearly too much risk to do that, and I pushed back. Now I wonder if that was a bigger deal than I realized," she said. "When the CEO acknowledged the team's efforts and named a few people at the next town hall meeting, I wasn't mentioned. I chalked it up to a large team with too many names to recall."

She sat up straighter in her chair. "A month later, my peer, who had less time on the team, was appointed lead on the next launch. When I asked my boss about it, he said, 'Elena, everyone gets a turn.' I felt reprimanded, like I was being selfish. I stopped asking about my promotion timing because I didn't want to upset him, even though it was way overdue. I figured that my hard work would show and pay off, given everything I continued to do. I'm exhausted. If he had an issue, why didn't he say anything?" she questioned with wet eyes.

I have often heard some version of this from professional women in mid-career. Suddenly, they woke up and saw that their external perception had shifted from successful to sidelined. Little things added up to an unannounced, invisible fall from grace. They felt unsteady on their feet, fretted about what to do next, and questioned the loyalty and advocacy that once felt so strong. They also felt frustration and resentment because they were given little to no direct communication about the issue, and they had to figure it out on their own while their confidence was rocked. To recover, they did what was always successful for them—work harder, play it safe, and prepare incessantly to get to the right answers and a better place.

Societal and familial expectations can inspire us to do great things. They also can unintentionally sideline who we really are and what we want. So many of our successful behaviors have an underbelly. Traits that initially fuel and work for us can begin to work against us in both our leadership and authenticity. I see it for myself more clearly now, having had decades to ponder my life, understand the research, and learn from the experiences of hundreds of students, colleagues, and friends.

On reflection, I see that so many of my own past actions were driven by my search for external validation or what others thought. This served to elevate me in the eyes of others yet at the same time cost me energy, stress, and my own interests. I inadvertently sidelined myself by my own and others' high expectations and what I thought were positive behaviors and attitudes. To be sure, like many women, I have felt challenged by external obstacles. I've faced a competitive boss frustrated by me as a rising star. I've worked for a manager whose actions showed he didn't think women should be in management. And I've dealt with the "queen bee" leader who thought there was room for only one woman in the group.

Systemic issues lock us out of success all too frequently. But I discovered I was also locking myself in from opportunity more often than not. I faced the mirrored door, operating in ways I thought would advance me. Little did I understand that I was marching in place and stuck in patterns that had once been positive but had now begun to limit my advancement. I soon found out I wasn't the only one. And neither are you.

As discussed in chapter 1, many girls adapt well to school, with its clear-cut rules, their ability to get the gold star from the teacher—and the knowledge of what will be on the test. The measures of success are clearly defined. Girls frequently excel in school, as can be seen by young women's academic achievements. But what happens when we try to excel without a rubric of what will be on the test? We learn too late that what gets rewarded changes between school and the workplace. Many work cultures and bias-filled behaviors limit women's advancements and need to be addressed. That said, until the workplace is fixed, we can't add to those inequities with any form of getting in our own way.

Clearly, our strategies for career success enable us to learn new skills, build meaningful connections with our colleagues, and cultivate experiences that can take us far. At the same time, we may unintentionally follow patterns that minimize our voices, opportunities, and real desires. When we mistakenly think we aren't ready enough, we sideline ourselves. We reduce our risk-taking, stand making, and sharing of our real selves. We so often tackle doubts by doing what we've been good at and were frequently rewarded for as children and young adults. But suddenly a situation shows us those same actions may even be blocking our momentum. These patterns have become silent self-saboteurs putting our future plans in peril. To address this, we must recognize what patterns work over the long term, reflect on our goals, and determine what actions we want to take.

Growing up, when we got perfect grades or were seen as perfect in any of our endeavors, it paid off, internally and externally. Our internally oriented perfectionism is grounded in intrinsic motivation and high standards that drive us to excel. Perfection feels inherent in who we are when it matches our love of what we do—our work, sport, home, business, or hobby. Our external, "other"-focused perfection includes the high standards we expect of others and the sky-high expectations we believe others expect from us. Researchers refer to this second type as "socially prescribed perfectionism."

When we are *preparing to perfection*, we strive for the right answers, 100 percent certainty, and always being the best. We deliver excellence repeatedly. It fuels our reputation and engagement in the work. It provides validation from others. We compare ourselves to others, and, when healthy, this leads to continuous improvement. When perfectionism becomes habitual, or the only way we know how to act, we may struggle to take risks and find it challenging to operate with incomplete information and/or to know when something is good enough. The workplace is full of such ambiguous situations. Navigating through uncertainty and ambiguity is part of being a leader.

Research indicates that the real issue with perfectionism is the fear of negative evaluation. This, combined with the double bind women face of struggling to be perceived as "just right"—demonstrating the expected "masculine" qualities of a leader while still having a warm, nurturing personality—can lead us to play it safe and avoid risk. This inhibits the development of leadership skills that are so critical to our advancement. Top leaders learn from taking actions with uncertain outcomes, such as recommending a transformational strategy, taking a challenging assignment, speaking up in a meeting, or confronting a conflict. So often our perfection is achieved by massive preparation, which helps us perform well, but we rely on it too much. When we cannot operate with less preparation or information, we struggle as we rise in the ranks and are required to make decisions that come with the risk of imperfect results.

When we are preparing to perfection, we fool ourselves into thinking that we can win a never-ending battle. But the fight isn't sustainable; more importantly, it's exhausting and prevents us from learning from mistakes, which is key to our growth as leaders. We stifle ourselves with self-criticism and hesitate around opportunities, and in doing so, we procrastinate taking action that advances us closer to our goals. A recent study of emerging adults shows that procrastination is highly correlated with fear of negative evaluation and perceived stress.

What's at Stake

"I'm not sure she is leadership material," the division leaders said to the department heads about their trusted director during the annual performance and potential assessment

The paradox is that
we can't apply the same
level of perfection that
we've always done but
we still believe that
we won't be successful
unless we are perfect.

meeting. "She's a hard worker and very smart, but we don't see her getting out of the weeds."

In two sentences, this ambitious thirtysomething woman's career at this company came into question.

We are frequently coached to prepare to perfection. We quickly learn the expectations around what is needed in a project, for a meeting, and to progress. Those who like to prepare relish the opportunity because it is squarely in their control. When we are well prepared, we've got the answers. Clients and senior leaders begin to count on us for solutions, knowing we've done the work. It's a major success factor, especially early in our careers, when getting things done well and assessing all the drivers, derailers, and details of a work product matter. We are acknowledged, appreciated, and asked again and again to participate in others' workstreams.

We soon learn to identify as the person who knows their stuff. We continue to take on more. We are respected as a doer, expert, project leader. We become successful within a team or organization. But that success has an underbelly when our perfectionism pigeonholes us as the preparer or the worker bee. It can lead to several perilous challenges.

First, we can find ourselves preparing for others to shine in the spotlight while inadvertently keeping ourselves hidden when the work is presented. Second, the workload can become overwhelming. We make the time in our day, and usually night, to prepare. Eventually, that preparation may dominate our time while other opportunities to grow are assigned elsewhere. Third, our preparation becomes our coping mechanism. When we don't have time to do the usual preparation, anxiety can kick in and we may avoid taking advantage of opportunities. Preparation gives us a boost, making us feel and appear competent. It gives us a bit more control and certainty in our areas of focus, increasing our chances of success. We rely on it.

We don't as readily see that our experience gets us there too, that we have grown our skills and competencies. We think we need more preparation than we do to be perfect in every meeting. Fourth, many women I have coached find they no longer have the time to do what they once did, but preparing to perfection is so ingrained that their fear grows. It steals the development of our skill to think on our feet, to be able to answer with a framework of what we know instead of the details of heavy-duty analysis.

Lastly, having a reputation of being prepared to perfection is not enough as we aspire to leadership roles. Leaders must be able to decide a course of action with limited information. When we always depend on hours of preparation, we don't learn how to move forward with partial information and the success or failure that results. The well-intentioned, over-prepared woman can easily get tagged as great to have on the team but not to lead it. Worse yet, our high standards may make us overly critical of those we are leading and developing. Instead of coaching others to excel, we may fall prey to micro-management, another perilous reputation.

If you see yourself in any part of the preparing to perfection strategy, you are not alone. Many successful women leaders have or continue to face this and find the courage to open the mirrored door. Research shows that women cope with perfectionism by managing the paradox of their internal expectations and their belief of what society, work, family expect. Through in-depth interviews of demographically diverse women, one study showed that perfectionism is experienced uniquely, and that women found their ways within the constraints of their cultural norms. While there are no cookie-cutter solutions, I recommend several areas to consider as you let go of or lighten up on this success strategy.

PREPARING TO PERFECTION: MANAGERS' CONSIDERATIONS

- When setting priorities with your direct report, clarify the deliverables and the rigor needed against each project so that she can better determine how much time and energy (and stress) to invest in it. Identify when a rough draft for input is enough as opposed to when an assignment needs a higher level of completion.

- Manage your direct report with a growth mindset. Recognize her progress with specifics, acknowledging her effort, development, and learning. Let her know the ways she is tracking well against your expectations or when she isn't given her time in the role. Share the growth you hope to see ahead by stating what you'll be looking for in the next six to twelve months. Discuss how her projects and priorities will enable that development.

- Model the way by sharing your own imperfections to create an environment of learning and idea generation. Reinforce that there is a time for perfectly thought-out recommendations and a time for rough ideas that might fall flat in the moment but could be the spark for ideas from others.

- Acknowledge and show appreciation for her smart risk-taking. See something and say something.

Reflect On Your Success

Years of preparing to perfection can build into a feeling that enough is enough. When you reflect on your quest for perfection and your purpose and goals, you will likely see that something's got to give. Let's be sure that isn't your career, your well-being, or the major contribution you make to your work and family. One way to recover from perfectionism is to adopt a growth mindset instead of a fixed one. Reflection is the key to getting there. It will help you objectively see your own progress and learning. If you find yourself overthinking something, dissect and reflect on the facts, your interpretation, and what else could be going on. Consider if there are actions you can take to move you out of rumination so you can let go of unproductive spinning.

When my female clients proactively make space to reflect on their successes over time, they recognize they have accomplished more, grown stronger, and progressed. I ask them to list what chances they took, what they learned, how they bounced back when something didn't go as planned, and what they'd do differently next time. They share their answers with me, surprised by their growth. This is why reflection is my number one recommendation for perfectionists and one of the best ways to assess, ignore the Inner Antagonist and everyday demands, and celebrate wins, losses, and insights. I encourage you to make it at least a weekly practice. Adding gratitude to your reflection can move you into a positive mindset.

Reframe the Roles

Being prepared to perfection is more likely to become perilous when our roles expand and grow. We may take on more responsibility in our company or at home and approach it with the same level of effort that has worked before. So frequently, more is added, and nothing is taken away. This calls us to operate more efficiently or take things off the list. This is a difficult part of the role transition we are experiencing. The paradox is that we can't apply the same level of effort toward perfection that we always have, but we still believe we won't be successful unless we are perfect. To disrupt ourselves, we must rethink perfection and dive into our expectations of the hats we wear. As we gain more accountability for people at work, we may need to force ourselves to delegate, and establish one-on-one check-ins on progress and outcomes. At home, our strategy may be reflecting on our vision of what gets done and who does it.

I asked one client to list all of the to-dos in her home and request that her partner do the same. It was shocking for them to see the dramatic difference in the length of their lists, and it opened more conversations about what they could do, divide, or ditch. Tiffany Dufu's book *Drop the Ball: Achieving More by Doing Less* is a call to working women to reconsider the standards to which we hold ourselves. While her manifesto is more focused on homes, the spirit of her message can be applied to our work life too. As we advance in our careers, we have to let go of some of the preparation that secured perfection for us in the past. We need to reframe our roles and the standards to which we deliver, balancing our own values and needs with what is most critically important in each role.

Plan for Action, Ask for Help

Many times, we resist deciding because we don't want to risk a bad outcome. If that resonates with you, consider creating a framework for your decision criteria that enables you to act. This could be as simple as determining, for example, that you can move forward if three of five assumptions are proven. Seek input and coaching from your manager so you can move forward with less-than-perfect information. When you receive a new request on top of a full plate, consider the time you can commit to it and ask if that will be sufficient for the level of risk involved in the work. If not, collaborate on how to reprioritize or offload other work. Engage others to help you make this shift.

I recommend that you talk to your boss about your deliverables. Work with them to identify the high-stakes work and where you can deliver more efficiently or delegate. I tell my clients and students: identify the As, Bs, and Cs. Negotiate how many As you can realistically handle with the excellence required, along with the level of completion of the Bs and Cs. This kind of conversation can help you create shared expectations of the work needed. You are no longer in school striving for a 4.0. It's time to focus the effort where it is most needed and match the remaining projects to the appropriate level of rigor. You may be thinking, *Everything is treated like an A in my workplace*. If so, that calls for a different conversation. As when you matched your course load to difficult content or how hard a semester would be, it's critical to set yourself up for success through courageous conversations that make for a sustainable work life. Delineating the A, B, and C projects is one way to do that. So often, our fear of messing up (FOMU), leads to fear of missing out (FOMO). When we hold back to avoid FOMU, we may trade off our shot at future opportunities. Later, we look back, wondering what opportunities could have been ours if we had let go of perfectionism and plunged into action that could have led to the next role. When we overprepare repeatedly, we then experience the FOMO on other ways we might be spending our time.

Get Real

Women are stereotypically thought to be more empathic, yet when we strive for perfection, we are rarely empathetic to ourselves. Get realistic about how hard you are on yourself and give yourself more compassion. My wish for you is that you let go of overdoing the preparation and begin to practice showing up less than perfect. Take one small, courageous step at a time followed by another, bigger one. Choose progress over perfection. Be prepared enough to progress. When you recognize that you are more ready than you thought and step through that mirrored door, you will realize you've got this. I'm betting you will soon see that you knew so much more all along. It's a journey, and you are no longer a solo traveler. Why wait?

KEY TAKEAWAYS

- When preparing to perfection, women habitually strive for absolute certainty, excellent delivery, and no risk.

- The power is that others count on our strong performance and reward us with promotions and accolades.

- The pitfall is that, in preparing to perfection, we become less flexible to operate differently when circumstances call for it.

- We see ourselves in the mirrored door when the stakes increase, the role changes, resources and time tighten, and we don't have the courage or experience to decide without the prep time we are used to.

- The peril is when our illustrious reputation of delivery is tarnished by a perception that lacks two key traits of leaders— skillful decision-making and risk-taking.

- The pivot is to understand that we *must* take risks to grow. We must reframe our thinking to a growth mindset of learning, recovering from mistakes, and celebrating progress over perfection.

JOURNAL PROMPTS

- How does being prepared to perfection currently help and/or hinder you?

- If you were focused on progress and growth over perfection, how might things be different for you?

- What's one thing you can do to try a new way of being?

6

Eagerly Pleasing

. . . .

"I've been absolutely terrified every moment
of my life—and I've never let it keep me
from doing a single thing I wanted to do."
GEORGIA O'KEEFFE

"THIS IS THE YEAR. We need to finally have our own Christmas here," I urged Ned, as we packed away the holiday decorations on New Year's Day.

"I know, I know. We've barely had a chance to enjoy the new house with all the traveling," he replied. "What do you think she will say?"

"I might lose my favorite-daughter-in-law status."

We finally had a mantel large enough to hold the Santa collection that had become the go-to gift from friends and my husband's seven siblings, and now we wanted to create the memories for our immediate family.

"She loves you. She'll understand. It will be fine." Ned carefully wrapped a glass bulb from our pre-kid travels in double bubble wrap. "We really have to handle these things delicately," he mumbled with tape between his teeth.

"You are right. That's true of the ornaments too." I smiled and wound the lights as though I was strangled. "I absolutely dread telling her."

As the months passed, the self-induced pressure mounted with anticipation of having "the conversation." We visited for Easter and saw how happy my mother-in-law was with the Easter egg hunt we held in her backyard.

"The girls will be three and five in December. Shouldn't we celebrate in our own house while they still believe?" I'd say repeatedly over the months, building up my justification. "I just wish we weren't the first to secede from the family. She's going to hate me."

When we are *eager to please*, we prioritize others and the greater good. We work collaboratively to build consensus and connections. In short, we keep the peace and ensure everyone is happy. In doing so, we are likeable, trusted, and, many times, the glue that holds groups or relationships together. We are adept at asking great questions and listening, reading the room, considering others' unexpressed views, and anticipating and offsetting an issue before it blows up. This way of operating makes us successful teammates and team leaders, especially in today's workplaces, where disengagement is high and a sense of belonging is low.

The upside of being eager to please can be diminished when we overdo it and leave ourselves out of the equation. The downside of this powerful success strategy is that we easily get hooked on being liked and hesitate to act in ways that we perceive would jeopardize our standing or relationships. We don't want to let others down, cause a problem, or seem selfish. We stand at the mirrored door, fearing judgment, and we hesitate to voice opposing opinions, prioritize our needs, confront conflict, or make unpopular decisions. Although being liked, trusted, and a consensus builder is valuable in our careers and leadership, we may also be perceived as non-confrontational and indecisive, which could be perilous to our future.

One of the most fraught relationships many women have is with their in-laws. It becomes the pinnacle of tension between wanting to please them and be liked in concert with the independence we crave to create a separate entity within the mothership. Even though I struck gold with the family I married into, I still struggled to draw the line between us and always felt judgment when we did. My husband? Not so much. It seemed so easy for him to decide and declare, whereas I was apologetic as I detailed our rationale at length. My need to please and struggle to set boundaries was not simply a familial issue.

I hear from so many women that it feels like we were born that way. Our rewarded orientation toward others shows up through our family life, education, and careers. We prioritize others and are loved for it. But this may lead to the neglect of our own priorities, needs, and aspirations. In the workplace, we become the person everyone wants on their team, yet may struggle to be seen as the ideal candidate to lead it. At its worst, our tendencies can register concerns that we avoid conflict, are indecisive, and are too soft on people. But when we learn to raise issues and build more ease in healthy disagreements and challenging conversations, we can leverage the much-needed power of our empathy, collaboration, and team-building skills, and stifle the negative effects of eager-to-please instincts. To do so, we need to risk speaking up and making tough calls, and we need to trust that we can do so while maintaining our relationships.

Hardwired to Please

"I have higher expectations than the rest of my study group. If I want it done well, I need to do it myself," my student Emma said in our coaching session.

"How is your schedule relative to theirs?" I asked.

"I'm just as busy. Possibly even more," she said. "I don't want to make a big deal out of this. It's fine. I don't know why I brought it up."

"What would that mean, if you didn't take on all the work? What's the real challenge for you?"

"I guess I don't want to keep doing all the work. But I don't want them to be mad at me." Emma furrowed her brow and paused as she grasped for words. "One person is stressed out because she doesn't have a job offer. Another is MIA because he is going through a breakup. It's a mess. I want everyone to get along and for us to get the A, but I don't want to rock the boat. It's just not worth it... I just can't help but feel like I am being taken advantage of. I am *so* tired of always having to do everything and take care of everyone." Emma's eyes glazed over as she reflected on the crossroads of taking care of herself amid a lifetime habit of keeping the peace and choosing others over herself.

Like Emma, most of us love to be liked. It feels good to please those around us. It is who we are. We learn this early and continue to uphold this role in many aspects of our lives, so much so that it becomes part of our identity. Shifting away from that perspective feels like it will cost too much, and this type of change is hard work emotionally. But the payoffs are long-lasting.

The sooner we recognize the impact of constant self-sacrifice on our lives and the exhaustion when it accumulates, the quicker we can begin to show up in a way that honors who we want to be. Sometimes we need to make some waves to get to a new place that is likely far more sustainable. My bet is that one small step will lead you to a greater ability to hold your ground, gain respect from others, and increase your peace of mind.

As mentioned in chapter 3, our society's bias is toward women who are communal, always looking out for the greater good. For all genders, that view is taught and ingrained early. Try as we might to be seen as both communal and agentic, we frequently find ourselves rooted in others' needs first and foremost. That orientation toward others enables us to make a positive impact in our households, classrooms, neighborhoods, teams, and companies. People also come to expect this orientation of us, which is an added layer of difficulty in stepping into our leadership identity. Plus, when our ingrained stereotype of what a leader is like is *unlike* us, imagining that we too could step into a leader's role is more challenging.

This tendency to please and prioritize others becomes our promise to the groups we are a part of, and it seeds cooperation. We learn to bring out the best in people. We have the emotional intelligence to understand people and anticipate and mitigate issues. We engage others in a friendly way that creates connection. We are counted on to do what's right for the broader community. Our relationships are harmonious, and our superpower is making everyone happy. People expect this of us, and we deliver on these powerful traits, at home, at work, in every arena. We become eager to please, and the payoff is big. We are many times adored.

The Peril of Being Eager to Please

Because we are hardwired to please, the notion of prioritizing ourselves or our own agenda creates a conflict with our identity and a fear that stops us at the mirrored door. We consider the energy it would take along with the possible fallout of a different approach, and keep our concerns or requests to ourselves. We wish those around us would simply know what we want. We've grown so used to our role that the idea of disagreement or asking for our fair share seems incredibly risky.

So often women are judged more harshly when they are less than altruistic, make mistakes, or are perceived as too aggressive. We run the risk of being shamed or mischaracterized for asking for what we want, being called entitled or worse. Common slang phrases like "resting bitch face" reinforce a discomfort with women being anything but smiling and happy. Is it any wonder that we sometimes hold back our expression of disappointment because it feels fraught with downsides?

There is another double bind at play: we may feel damned if we continue in our people-pleasing ways and damned if we change them and let everyone down.

I care enough about you and your future to tell you that the disease to please has a dark side that accumulates over time and sneaks up on us, impacting our careers, relationships, and psyche. The paradox of pleasing others is that it feels so risky to walk through that mirrored door and away from the image others have of us that we miss the real risk: losing ourselves in others' needs and never getting our own met. Such relationship concessions can add up and may aggregate into greater frustrations or underlying anger. We can feel taken for granted, annoyed at always having to play a role, or simply forgotten as our needs are left behind.

EAGERLY PLEASING:
MANAGERS' CONSIDERATIONS

- Acknowledge your direct report's relationship-building skills and their impact on the team and business. Help her see that her tendency is valuable and she is more than a nice, kind person. Remind her of her influence—for example, how she turned around a difficult discussion or motivated a group of people to do something challenging. In doing so, you are reinforcing the strengths of these soft skills that are sometimes underestimated.

- Create a safe, open environment that enables healthy debate and disagreement. Show that it is okay to raise issues, say no, and ask for what you need. Encourage when this happens.

- Model how you address conflict while maintaining relationships. Openly discuss the challenge of addressing issues while maintaining connection.

- Clarify roles and expectations with the full team, so that accountability is clear. Support her in assessing a sticky situation and collaborate on next steps when she needs support in managing conflict.

- Delegate your high-value initiatives across the team. Ensure that additional to-dos are also split equally. Consider whether in the past you have assigned her to projects or tasks that don't fit her role or advance her performance results or promotion candidacy. If she has been asked to and taken on too much of the office housework, address the situation.

Change Is an Inside Job

My hope is that you discover what enables you to thrive. And my greatest wish is that you practice saying no or pushing back, one small step at a time. A first step is to know what you need.

When we hold our needs inside, we don't set ourselves up for success. We also construct hidden expectations that others in our work and life are unable to meet, seeding our own disappointment—we somehow expect the people in our lives to be mind-readers. Of course, I wish I didn't have to tell my partner or boss what makes me feel valued, my number one need. But if I keep that need to myself, I increase the chance that it will not get met.

I teach my students and clients that "needs" are the requirements for us to be at our best. When needs are met, they are invisible. When they aren't met, something seems wrong. It's hard to pinpoint what is happening, but we are usually bothered by something that is not being fulfilled. If we can ask for that, we increase our chances of thriving.

For many women, boundary setting is difficult. It is particularly challenging when you want to please everyone and preserve relationships. While we know rationally that we need to establish boundaries, we frequently hesitate because of the response we might get. We fear we will inconvenience others, or be seen as selfish or mean. Though we can't control other people's reactions, the stories we imagine range from an awkward interaction to missed opportunities to a catastrophic collapse of a job or friendship.

I find it helps to consider the worst that can happen. This questioning cuts through what we conjure and helps us recognize that our worst fear is typically not very likely. For example, you might get pushback and then need to reassert your boundary. Many times, it ends at the firmness you exhibit. If not, then

The sooner we recognize the impact of constant self-sacrifice on our lives and the exhaustion when it accumulates, the quicker we can show up as who we want to be.

go down a layer: Is their reaction really going to damage the relationship? Is this really true? When we draw a firm line, we may meet disappointment but usually find ourselves being heard and respected. We set the stage for more balanced give-and-take and avoid being a pushover. But if that is not the reaction, then go deeper and consider: What does that mean? It may indicate something about the quality of relationship. Do you really want a relationship that doesn't allow you to speak your mind and take care of your needs?

Almost every student, client, and colleague who struggles with boundaries excels in relationships. They don't see that their strong ties can withstand disagreement, negotiations, and the word "no." They are adept relationally, yet they may be scared to broach difficult subjects and draw a line in the sand. They aren't aware of how they are truly thought of and how others likely value being treated directly and transparently.

If this topic resonates with you, I suggest you practice the following framework: the Three Cs of Brave Boundary Setting. Do this in the easiest of conditions so that you can keep at it as the stakes grow higher. This framework helps amazing, unassuming women with rock-solid relationships (that they don't always realize they have in abundance). It leverages their strengths to enable them to have the necessary talks they're avoiding.

First, you must know what you want and what's at stake, and be ready to go for it. This requires a courageous conversation to ensure your need is met. Start with the smallest need you can think of and then try one bigger, and so on.

1. **Clarify.** Begin by clearly stating the boundary. Make it a declaration with commitment. And avoid using minimizing words or phrases like "We are thinking about..." or "I kind of want to..." In this step, don't add questions like "What do you think?" unless you are negotiating. Keep your reasons brief so as not to

undo your resolve or get talked out of your decision. Keeping it brief focuses the discussion on how to handle the boundary, not if it should be in place. Two examples of a clearly stated boundary are: 1) "I'm not able to take on that project given my current workload and other commitments," and 2) "I won't be able to make it to your get-together."

2. Connect. After stating your boundary, pause to listen for the other person's response. You likely have a lot of empathy for others. Use that gift and your understanding of the other person here to acknowledge the impact your choice might have. This is a moment of genuine appreciation and understanding of the other person. Connect with compassion, not apology or sympathy. Share your thoughts and be open to their reaction. While you can't control their response, you can learn from it, and that may help in considering next steps. You could say: 1)"I know this is disappointing, as I know you have a full plate and this will take a lot of time and effort," or 2) "I know you want to have a great gathering and a full house."

3. Collaborate. Next, offer support in ways that help the other person focus and take the lead on what is next. It is critical that they, not you, be on point for the future. It might help to ideate around the options or what is needed to move forward. Examples here are: 1)"I can suggest a few names of people in the XYZ department who might have time to project manage the initiative. I'm happy to brainstorm other options," and 2) "I look forward to joining you at one of your next events. Let me know if you'd like me to pass along the invitation to someone else."

Making the Shift Stick

. . . .

In Emma's case, we focused on what she could control: her reluctance to raise the issue with her study group and the creation of an approach she could use in school and in her future job. First, she had a heart-to-heart with the group that opened the door to a lot of unexpected, rich dialogue. They reset the roles and approach for the next assignment. Most important was her relief that her actions led to a better way. Though she had struggled with the thought of bringing up her concerns, her careful planning gave her the courage to take the first steps.

As she starts with new project teams, she now adds an important step. She initiates a discussion and asks each person their current situation and personal goal within a project. She goes first and communicates where she can most contribute and learn. This surfaces gaps in schedules, expected outcomes, and skills to develop or leverage. It sets up shared and divided tasks, assigned roles, and any challenges the team may face. While Emma originally created this for school projects, it has become her signature approach to new consulting projects within her firm. She has broken through the hidden barrier. Instead of feeling taken for granted, she creates proactive solutions that offset her instinct to take it all on herself. With practice, this has become part of how she shows up and leads. While she once feared the conflict communicating her concerns might create, she now wonders, "What was I waiting for?"

Facing the Fear

. . . .

Family relationships can be among the most challenging, especially when it comes to merging family expectations. In my own case, I ruminated for months over my mother-in-law's possible reaction to our holiday plans and imagined a catastrophic break in our strong relationship. When we finally told her, she shocked us.

"What took you so long? I've been waiting for one of you to have Christmas at your own house. We did that too. Of course, you'd want the girls to celebrate and await Santa in their own beds. I get it."

From that day forward, we had a new level of understanding and honesty. It showed me how much time I had wasted being worried and taught me the value of understanding my own needs and fears regarding the risk of letting others down.

Years later, I learned to use the Three Cs of Brave Boundary Setting—clarify, connect, and collaborate—in all areas of my life. When I find myself slipping from reflection to rumination, I set an alarm, allowing myself an hour to obsess, and then it's time to move on. When a colleague or client has a major upset, I give them the same advice, suggesting they take until Sunday noon to worry, but then it's time to move on and limit the unproductive thoughts that rob us of our peace of mind.

My wish for you is that you understand whether you are eager to please and, if you are, when you first learned this. How has it helped you and where does it limit you in the short and long terms? Consider your relationships objectively. Be honest. Can they withstand you setting boundaries, a difference of opinion, or a debate? Think about people you respect for the way they balance their give-and-take. How could your evolution inspire others to do the same? Lastly, why not raise this with those closest to you? What about the people you work with day-to-day? How might you model the way for others in your life? Don't forget all the upsides and power in this success strategy. Get ready to rebalance, with more of you in the equation.

KEY TAKEAWAYS

- Eager-to-please women prioritize others and the greater good, listen collaboratively, build consensus, and keep the peace.

- The power is that we influence others, making them better, more engaged, and more likely to operate well as part of a group.

- The pitfall is when we become so "other"-oriented that we neglect our own needs, interests, and views.

- We face the mirrored door when we aren't pleased, disagree, want our own needs met, want to confront conflict, or wish to say no—and we hesitate because we don't want to risk relationships. We quiet our own voice, and sometimes resentment and frustration grow.

- The peril is that we are seen as too soft, without strong opinions, and unable to make tough decisions or have difficult conversations.

- The pivot is to seek respect over likeability, learn to set boundaries, and take small steps to raise issues, our voices, and conflicts. Employees want people-driven leaders. We must leverage our eagerness to please and lead without forgetting ourselves.

JOURNAL PROMPTS

- In what areas of your life do you advocate for others? What enables you to do that?

- What would it be like to trust your relationships enough to risk saying no, raising an issue, or asking for what you want? Commit to trying one of these actions in one situation this week.

- What boundary could make a meaningful difference for you? Write a script for sharing that boundary using the Three Cs of Brave Boundary Setting.

7

Fitting the Mold

. . . .

"There is power in allowing yourself to
be known and heard, in owning your unique
story, in using your authentic voice."
MICHELLE OBAMA

"**I** **THINK YOU** should take those home during your lunch hour," my boss suggested.

"Wait, what? They just arrived," I responded, the glow draining from my face.

"If the other zone manager sees that you got roses, he's going to think you're practically engaged. This could cost you the promotion to district manager."

"I'm nowhere near engaged. And even if I were, I could still relocate."

"He'll assume otherwise and not take the chance. You should be next on the list, and he's likely to have the next opening. I don't want to see you miss your opportunity," he said. "It's your call. I'd do it. You live only ten minutes away."

I reflected on the women who had moved up the ranks before me. In the days when moving to different markets and roles was the way promotions worked, they were all single. The few married women and absence of moms in sales leadership told me all I needed to know. I'm embarrassed now to say that I took the flowers home to avoid the risk of being seen as making a career-limiting move.

In addition to my silence about my personal future, I learned the importance of a "game face" from another manager. Based on his feedback and coaching, I learned to mask my disappointment when I was caught off guard with a difficult question, received blunt biased feedback, or an unplanned problem occurred at a group meeting. I engineered a positive, unflappable exterior that garnered praise. As the priority projects and promotions followed, I was thrilled. My advocates continued to groom me for more responsibility, and that reinforced their selection and support. I was a hungry go-getter who never made a fuss and was always up for the next challenge, no matter how impossible it might be. To succeed, I delivered what my managers expected and directed, and I did so willingly, which gave me membership in their club.

When we *fit the mold*, we flex our agility to gain entry, fit in quickly, and follow the cultural norms to build familiarity and connection with the team. We add an "easy" diversity to the organization when we seem just like them, only different. We harmonize with the existing team seamlessly and thus advance. While that specific expectation—"single equals promotable"— that I faced has evolved, the pressure for women to conform to the latest standards continues.

Under the Spotlight

When we enter workplaces as one of the few or the only, we instantly feel the burden of fitting in. When we are in the minority in a group, our internal sensor goes off whenever we perceive we are under a spotlight because of our differences.

The risk of that glare tells us we need to blend into the crowd. As outsiders, we hone the skills to read the situations surrounding us and adapt to adhere to the group norms. Bending ourselves to belong begets praise, elevates our potential, and makes things easy for the rest of the team. It works for us to follow others' leads and laws—the promotions and possibilities are the rewards for our efforts.

The promise of this success strategy is that we become astute observers, knowing what does and doesn't work, assimilating and learning to speak the language, dress the part, and behave within the boundaries of an organizational culture. We strive to be and be perceived as the ideal worker, with a relentless commitment to work without outside distractions. Being a workplace chameleon gives us great agility to build relationships in a variety of situations and environments. Our reputation and credibility with the majority grows and the payoff is acceptance and a sense of belonging in the short term.

"I began to have one personality at work and another in my life. It was exhausting and confusing," said an MBA student, confiding in me about her previous job. As Ekta gained management responsibilities, she became the only woman and person of color in her tech company's top one hundred leaders group. "I enjoyed the work and was good at it, but I never felt I could really be myself," she said. As a woman in her late twenties, she was driven to succeed at work but questioned the divide between who she needed to be to command respect at work and the friendly, casual, fun-loving person she was at home. She explained to me:

As my career progressed, I began to be acknowledged in larger group meetings as an example of excellence and hard work. I dreaded the praise heaped on me and thought others might too. I just wanted to do my job and be myself, not someone held up as the standard. My sense was that they didn't have a diverse group of people to choose from and I became the one to mention. The C-suite thought this was valuable praise, but I began to feel worried that one misstep could sink the opportunity for other women or people of color. Worse yet, I was tapped to lead the employee resource group, as if I had the time. I became the go-to person to teach others about diversity. And how could I say no?

I'm no expert and only had my own experience to share. I felt pressured and was burnt out by the added burden and stress that came with my gender, race, and culture. The real me was nowhere to be seen and I no longer belonged. I eventually quit. When I look back on my time there, I grew a lot, but I don't think they ever really knew me.

The Peril of Fit

When we position ourselves to match company culture, we increase our chances of success. But we may also stretch too far from who we really are. Many times, the advice from colleagues as well as what we perceive is valued by the culture drive us to contort ourselves, sometimes beyond recognition. We unwittingly construct an unsustainable, exhausting habit that can rob us of our authenticity. Along the way, the company doesn't get the benefit of our true diverse experience and point of view. When we hide who we are, our stress, dissatisfaction, and disengagement increase. We sense we don't belong. We may worry about the repercussions if our true self were to be revealed.

When we fit the mold, we face the mirrored door and assess that who we are is not what they want. And we stack up the evidence to support that belief. We begin to see less of ourselves and more of who we think they want to see. We capture a distorted image that will best do the job and help us belong. A recent *Harvard Business Review* article referred to this as a maladaptation called "I need to fit in to rise." Through their

interviews, the authors found that women feel pressure to conform, give up parts of their identity, and edit their behavior to
advance their careers. When we hide our true selves or limit
what others see, it is like putting a chain lock on the mirrored
door. We partially reveal our true selves, but the promise of who
we fully are remains a well-kept secret known to few.

Most of us work in environments that weren't created for
us. Our intersectional identities, meaning the way we identify
in multiple aspects like gender, race, sexual orientation, ability,
religion, and so on, and our lived experiences are not recognized by our colleagues and vice versa. The workplace becomes
a mirrored maze for those who were not in the majority when
the rules were set. Is it any wonder that we internalize the
many cues to be a certain way to meet our goals? Those signals
may be provided directly, as with my boss, or they may come
from "reading the tea leaves" and our expert detection of what
is expected. We might reflect inward, question ourselves, our
safety, and why we got the attention or the job.

The learned, highly successful ability to adapt can become
perilous for women in two ways. First, like Ekta, we may grow
tired of playing by the outdated rules of others. This form of
code-switching, where we adopt the rules or codes of a company instead of our own, can impact both our work and our
mental wellness.

Second, when we show who we really are, others may perceive us as less promising than they previously thought. I
frequently hear from women that fitting the mold helped
them achieve and grow at first, but this growth was short-lived,
especially as they stepped into and wanted to show their true
selves. Sometimes the novelty of our presence wears off and our
push for an agenda of inclusion or another change is greeted as
problematic, especially for Black women. Kecia Thomas coined
the "pet to threat" phenomenon, where Black women are valued and supported early on by management, but that attitude

changes as they grow more competent and confident. When women grow too big for the mold, it becomes harder for the organization. Instead of it welcoming new thinking and healthy debates, its underlying biases put women's careers in peril.

FITTING THE MOLD: MANAGERS' CONSIDERATIONS

- Acknowledge how diverse thinking and perspectives help the team and company be more innovative and increase the chance of meeting customers' needs.

- Consider how your employees from underrepresented groups might be affected by pressures to fit in. To succeed, do women need to fit a mold or is the mold expanding or breaking to transform the organization?

- Review employee surveys to see how diverse employees rate the company and management. Are women and people of color feeling included—like they belong, are respected, and have a future path there? How might policies and practices need to change to deliver on the promise of diverse organizations?

- Remember that no one group is a monolith. Avoid putting the weight of diversity, equity, and inclusion (DEI) initiatives on the shoulders of women and other underrepresented groups. Share the workload, credit the work in performance reviews, and encourage real allyship.

- Acknowledge and applaud input, collaboration, and authenticity. Create safety in the growing pains of organizational change and the freedom to express how you and your company will get better. Model that you and the team are all learning.

When Fit Goes Rogue

It's human nature to choose to be around others like us. In a *New York Times* opinion piece, Kellogg School of Management professor Lauren Rivera reveals that cultural fit has become a new form of discrimination that suppresses demographic and cultural diversity. Hiring for fit makes it easier for the majority to relate, mitigates preconceived notions or biases, and reduces the occurrences of something we all fear: awkward moments. Companies increasingly want diversity but don't always know how to value and encourage it. They haven't always assessed the systemic processes and approaches that allow for different people to thrive. Too often, a lack of familiarity and similarity is deemed "not a fit" during hiring decisions.

The fit bias continues later in women's careers too. One study showed that the conditioned view of leadership in a masculine model negatively impacts women's longer-term careers. Yet another study showed that women received substantially lower "potential" ratings despite getting higher job performance ratings.

"I'm just not sure of her leadership potential" and "I'd like to see more gravitas" are uttered all too often in executive sessions designed to assess long-term career planning and promotions. As a leader in several of these sessions over the years, I've found getting past these subjective comments difficult. The predominantly male executives seemed to hold an unconscious bias that "something wasn't right" when assessing a high performer who didn't look or act like typical, usually male leaders.

When we position ourselves to match company culture, we increase our chances of success. But we may also stretch too far from who we really are.

Breaking the Bias

Women, especially women of color, must deal with the dynamic of outperforming others while coming up short for the next promotion. It fuels us to prepare to perfection and fit the mold. We continuously try to prove ourselves and be seen and recognized. This dynamic motivates many to "play the game to change the game." Maybe then we can stop trying to fit in and begin to break the mold.

Ruchika Tulshyan, author of *Inclusion on Purpose: An Intersectional Approach to Creating a Culture of Belonging at Work*, suggests that to truly gain the benefits of diversity and build belonging, organizations should *add* to the mold. She sees the quest for "culture fit" as coded bias: it signals fit with the existing culture as opposed to searching for something additive. She highlights the need for organizations to understand their biases and systemic issues, and create psychological safety to enable risk-taking. To date, the onus has been placed on women's shoulders, but organizations also need to open up the path for everyone to succeed. It may start with us, as there is no better time to push for more change in organizations than ever before.

Did They Hire the Real Me?

"I did what I said I wanted to do with my MBA—shift into health care," Pam, my student, shared with a huge smile and bright eyes. After talking about her career path with great excitement, she pursed her lips.

"What else is on your mind?" I asked.

"I really want to wear my natural hair when I start, but I don't know how that will fly," she whispered. "I would never have even considered this at my past firm. And I didn't see anyone else doing that during my summer internship at the new company."

"What does it mean for you to be able to do that?" I queried.

"It makes me feel like I made it. Like they really want me for who I am," she said. "I'm so tired of looking like someone else and playing small when I have so much more in me."

"How might others respond and how much does their response matter to you?"

"To be honest, if they hired me for my hairdo, then that's their problem. I can still show them how good I am. I have this crazy dream that all the other Black women will do the same. It's silly and I can't believe I told you that," she said, returning to the bubbly student I enjoyed in class that quarter. "I'm scared and excited rolled into one, but I think I'm going to go for it."

I saw Pam a year later when she was back for MBA intern recruitment. What a pleasure to see her joy as she stopped by to say hello. I couldn't help but blurt out, "I love your hair!"

She smiled. "They do too. It's a journey, but they do too."

Staying True

"Authenticity" has become buzzworthy in recent years. Articles and books promote it while others question if anyone really wants to see their coworkers' authentic selves. That said, there is a continuum from "let it all hang out" authenticity to fitting the mold with an inauthentic self. The questions to ask yourself include:

- How can I be closer to who I am and succeed here?
- What is the benefit and cost to showing up more authentically in this workplace?
- What actions indicate an open engagement of differences?

Herminia Ibarra authored a classic article in the *Harvard Business Review* called "The Authenticity Paradox." She has a different take on the long-held business adage of "fake it till you make it" that has frustrated many of those who reject the idea of being fake to get our way. Ibarra's thesis is that we can grow only if we put ourselves in new, sometimes awkward situations where we may feel like we don't belong or don't have the skills to succeed. She argues for expanding beyond what has felt authentic in the past to become more. I agree with her, and I would add that the individual challenge is to determine how we can learn and evolve from new, sometimes trying situations while not twisting ourselves beyond recognition. We are all given the advice to get out of our comfort zone. We do this all the time through education, new companies, new roles, and so on. My advice to my students is to expand. The confidence to be who you are comes after you summon the courage to show up more fully. How and where can you stretch yourself without breaking?

Standing out and pushing back takes courage, especially in the face of a culture of conformity. We must bring awareness to who we truly are, with all our strengths, where we want to go, and what we uniquely offer. The pivot is to stay true to ourselves at our core, understand the value we bring, and identify where we might need to dial up or down some aspect to grow and impact the culture we are in, or find elsewhere.

This pivot also requires you to know what you are up for at this phase of your career and life. You may find that being your more authentic self in one company is an uphill battle. Perhaps you see potential and love the role, the product, and growth prospects. If you believe they are open to change, you might want to pioneer and model the way forward. You can inspire others as you show them what authenticity looks like. You'll need to assess your own willingness to be an agent of change and to understand the company's commitment to transformation, the resources and support they will put behind it, and the realistic odds of change. At other times in your career, you may not want to be the driver and instead want to join a team that requires less cultural work. If that is where you are at, then it will be critical to dig deep to know what you are walking into next. Get perspectives from multiple angles and search for examples that confirm and disconfirm your view to be sure you are going in objectively, with both eyes open.

If you want to be more yourself at work, you must know who you are. One of the best ways to do that is to identify your top values. These are the things that matter most to you at your core. They are like the compass that guides your actions, what you care about, and what feels wrong when violated.

Tasha Eurich writes that only 10–15 percent of people are truly self-aware. In her book *Insight*, she identifies two parts of self-awareness, our internal and external awareness. To build our internal awareness, we must understand our values, strengths, passions, and what made us who we are. To build our external awareness, we must understand our impact on others. Perhaps we sense the effect we have on others. The best way to do this is to get feedback. As discussed in chapter 3, getting good at receiving feedback can reinforce what's working for us and where we might be getting in our own way.

The more we know who we truly are, the more we can consciously consider how we might show up fully as opposed to showing up how we perceive our organization expects us to. Think like an anthropologist in assessing a company's expectations, rewards, and examples of success. Does that intersect with who you are and your values? The greater the overlap, the more likely you are to thrive within the existing culture. The smaller the overlap, the more work to be done and the greater likelihood that you'll need to be an agent of change. Many people build careers as changemakers that transform cultures.

The power is in knowing who you are and assessing who they—the company, leadership, and team—are so you can choose. Given what you feel you have to do to fit the mold, can you still be effective, engaged, and growing? Will you need to give up too much of yourself? Said another way, can you fit without selling your soul? Can you fit comfortably now to rise and eventually drive the change needed in yourself and your organization? Transforming a culture can be incredibly rewarding. Leading others along the way can be one's greatest legacy.

Hidden in Plain Sight

"I'm proud of my family but I felt a lot of shame because they were not accepted in many places," Teresa shared. "When I joined a big tech company, I didn't want people to know my background. I even softened my accent," she confessed. "I regret it now, but it was easier than drawing attention to how different I was from everyone else. At work, everyone assumed I was white; they didn't see me as a Latina."

"How is it for you now?"

"It is stressful."

"How so?"

"I saw a young manager from work at an extended family party. She looked shocked and then excited to see me in my real life. The next week at work, she looked puzzled when she saw me.

"When I said hi, she asked me if I have to act like 'them' and she pointed to the row of management offices. I can't stop thinking about our conversation and her disappointed face."

"What are your thoughts?"

"I've hidden who I am and I'm tired of that. What message am I sending to young women like her?" she said. "I'm starting today to be who I am."

I hope you will do the same. For the sake of our careers and all those who follow us, let's do the hard work of taking chances, modeling the way, and challenging fit bias, and create new molds of what leadership looks like.

KEY TAKEAWAYS

- Fitting the mold enables women to ease entry into organizations and fit in quickly.

- Its power is that we are agile. We know how to follow the cultural norms and connect with the team.

- The pitfall is that we don't show our full selves or opinions, robbing the group of truly knowing us and our diverse thinking.

- We face the mirrored door when we doubt our seat at the table, wonder if they value us for who we are, and feel stress at the thought of showing people who we truly are.

- Fitting the mold becomes perilous because it is exhausting. Keeping up the pretense of a "real self" and "work self" is unsustainable.

- The pivot is to tap into courage to share more of ourselves at our organization, or to find a different organization where we can be more authentic. Once we take a chance, we'll likely take more and model the way for others.

JOURNAL PROMPTS

- Does your company inadvertently have a mold that you must fit to be successful? How is that mold expanding, breaking, or contracting?

- Brainstorm how you might communicate what you need from your boss, team, or self to show up as you are, more integrated and real. What's one thing you could do to advance that?

Working Pedal to the Metal

*"Here's to strong women. May we know them,
may we be them, may we raise them."*
UNKNOWN

"**YOU ARE WORKING** your way out of a job," said Liz, one of the cofounders at the start-up Suzanne had joined several months earlier. After fifteen years in large consumer packaged goods companies, Suzanne relished the opportunity to join a growing company in the health food space.

She knew something wasn't working, and Liz's unsolicited comment confirmed it. Suzanne had been so busy "getting shit done" at the pace she was used to in her previous corporate career. Her long hours of preparation and extra effort "dotting all the i's and crossing all the t's" wasn't yielding her usual results. She was hitting her head against the wall with the team and worked even harder to motivate them. The people were great, the market opportunities were big, and she had the experience to make an impact.

"What gives?" Suzanne wondered aloud to her husband, who knew the team. Liz's observation burned deeply but provoked Suzanne to step back. She decided to speak about the problem with the other partner, her direct boss, Joe, who welcomed the conversation.

"You're moving too fast for us," he shared, and gave her examples.

"I'm trying to deliver on this new launch."

"You are acting like you are command central. They don't like that. You've got to bring them along. You have a maniacal focus that might be a little scary to them."

Though she was shocked, it was a moment of truth. And with that clarity, Suzanne realized she had two choices. She could declare the company wasn't a fit and move on, or she could (wisely) consider whether she had something to learn there. She decided to set aside her disappointment, lose the ego she had about the right way to do things based on her corporate experience, and learn from the founders and the team.

Suzanne called me to work with her on what she called "operation do-over"—a reset of her product launch team leadership. Her spunky attitude and endless energy enabled her to stay positive through the difficult feedback from the team.

"I thought I was always seen as a team player, and I don't get why they don't see me the way I see myself," she said.

"What are you doing to get to know the team and bring them along in your vision?" I asked.

Suzanne contemplated the question. "I've shown them I'm a hard worker with high standards. But... they don't really know me. And I don't know them. I guess I jumped right in and skipped a step."

Suzanne's passion to push herself and others creates results but sometimes leaves others in her dust. She hadn't seen this in the past because her team members knew her and one another better and may have operated similarly. Suzanne and I outlined an off-site agenda to kick off "operation do-over," including the "get to know you" part, the strategies to meet the launch, and a discussion of what they needed from each other to make it happen. Suzanne learned from this experience that her zealous approach led her to work in a silo and not pull others along. I challenged her to listen with a lens of curiosity to get out of the judgment she felt when someone wasn't as aggressive as she was. We also worked on her communications about who she is. She began to offset the possible reaction to her high-energy, assertive style by sharing that she was passionate to get this product into consumers' hands. She gave others the permission and urged them to give feedback if she went overboard and missed what mattered to them. Lastly, she was burnt out from years of a constant hard-working approach. She found the time to pause and relax, recharge, and reflect.

"I put my head down, got humble, and became much more vulnerable," she told me a year later. Her intuition and the guts to listen and learn at this defining moment kept her at the company, where she launched another highly successful product line and eventually became the CEO. She not only learned from her new colleagues but also significantly influenced the organization through their high-growth phase, which required much more discipline and speed as the organization, customer base, and business grew larger. This experience was foundational to her career and led to her to be founder, CEO, investor, and/or board director of multiple entrepreneurial ventures in the broader industry.

When we embrace a *pedal to the metal* approach, we work tirelessly to drive results, have a high capacity for work, and keep our eye on the prize. We have the identity of a winner, a striver, a forward-looking leader. The promise we offer to our workplaces is that we are ready for challenging goals and will do what it takes to achieve them. Those with this tendency usually have high competencies and are constantly improving themselves and those around them, whether they like it or not. When there is a difficult, uncertain change needed, management assigns someone who exhibits these qualities because they will drive themselves and their teams far. For those with this success tendency, they feel seen when asked to step up to something they've never done before. They believe they can pull it off and have much evidence to support that from past successes. Others count on them for their genuine interest and open readiness to take on more and get things done.

The Peril of Working Pedal to the Metal

Working with a pedal-to-the-metal tendency, you keep your foot on the gas. You power through and move quickly, sometimes leaving others in your dust. The peril of this approach involves relationships, with others and yourself. You might try so hard that you lose balance and neglect the fine balance of your colleagues' needs and your own. Suzanne's tunnel vision led her to miss some key insights that were needed for the launch. But her single-minded dedication to the deliverables expanded when she learned more about her team and their areas of expertise and opinions on the project.

Hard-charging behavior may be seen as results-oriented but is incongruous to expectations of our gender, and so we may experience resistance to our ideas and direction, especially if we skip the team-building that can create a foundation of trust and connection. As we learned in earlier chapters, research shows us that a more aggressive leadership style conveys the competency we expect of leaders and men, but it challenges the biased shared expectations that women be warm and likeable.

On the surface, this tendency appears like action as if we are walking through the mirrored door. In reality, we are running in place when we work in a silo and don't bring the team along with us. We can exhaust ourselves and suddenly realize that we can run on fumes for only so long. Our relentless pursuit of our goals can impact our well-being, mental health, and internal balance. When we identify as a winner, we may be defensive in the face of feedback and less coachable, and have outsized reactions when we get bad news. A fear of failure can be fuel to push even harder to achieve results. Our behavior may be so ingrained that we don't recognize the signs in our body that we are burnt out. I frequently hear from women who tend to put the pedal to the metal that they have enormous energy for weeks and months followed by getting very sick, as though only the illness can slow them down enough to increase their level of self-care.

Slow Down to Speed Up

If you find your preference for a pedal-to-the-metal approach is wearing down your relationships, you may need to slow down so that you and your team can speed up together once you've pulled them along with you and collectively set the pace. This may feel incongruent with your standard approach. I encourage you to take on a mini-challenge and experiment with slowing down your pace. My hope is that it will sync you up with others, motivate them to carry on and speed up, and join you in the work and enthusiasm for the goals. Slowing down brings balance to the amazing energy you have for everything in your life. Pause your default approach and process for the sake of your relationships with others. If you sense that you are driving all decisions, perhaps because of constructive feedback telling you so, then it may be time to stop and listen to others, to give colleagues the opportunity to contribute and make your collective work better. These steps may come naturally to some. For others, I suggest engineering the process. For example, you can use your project management ability and strategic thinking to craft a shared agenda that allows for a healthy debate that includes all project contributors. You might ask for comments, questions, areas of disagreement, or votes to be submitted in writing. You can use polls in virtual meetings and Post-its or index cards in person to surface what is going unsaid. The group can then discuss the merits of each idea. The goal here is to build collaboration, candor, and contributions as you take in the points of view of others and let that input influence the work. I encourage you to set a short time limit to keep the interactions engaging and effective.

Offset the Bias

Women with pedal-to-the-metal mindsets and behaviors are seen as highly competent and leaderlike. This rubs up against society's ingrained bias to expect warmth in women above all. When a woman's competence is more prominent than her warmth, it creates a cognitive dissonance—our experience doesn't match our expectations. As we learned in early chapters, when people of all genders think "leader," they most often think "man." When they think warmth, "other"-orientation, and likeability, they think "woman." We may struggle to be seen as likeable, and this may hurt our ability to get things done. We might overthink a project or a sticky situation, hesitating in front of the mirrored door.

My advice is not to change the amazing results-driven leader you are but to show more of yourself and your motivations to

My advice is not to change the amazing results-driven leader that you are but to show more of yourself and your motivations to others.

others. Understanding that gendered assumptions and the double bind we face are, unfortunately, alive and well, we must offset them by considering how to manage the backlash, thinking and acting strategically, and by learning from each other.

I work with an amazing professor who is tough as nails. She is aware that she can be one of the most challenging teachers students face, and that word gets around about her classroom rules, grading, and exacting standards. She opens her class by saying, "I'm possibly the toughest teacher you will have here. I'm going to be in your face and hold you to all of the work I assign. I do this because I'm passionate about this subject and know that my class will make you incredibly strong in this content. I want you to be your best, and I'll help you get there. Now what questions do you have about and for me?" Her introduction tells the class who she is, lets them know what to expect, and counterbalances judgment. She shifts her students from possible dislike or resistance to trust and respect. The only "B word" used to describe her is "bold."

Another helpful tactic is to build your relationships by asking for feedback in advance, as Suzanne did. This may establish connection, show you want to improve, and give permission for others' input. Assuming they take you up on it, you will learn when you need to dial up listening or dial down your high energy and commanding nature to better align with and engage others.

WORKING PEDAL TO THE METAL: MANAGERS' CONSIDERATIONS

- Acknowledge a woman's drive, efforts, and ability to get the job done.

- Coach her development in the areas of collaboration, delegation, and motivating a team for high performance. Teach her how to motivate others through setting a vision and co-developing the plan to get there.

- Clarify your expectations around workload, face time, response time, and so on. Share details about your transition from individual contributor to leader of others. Talk about how to let go, lean on others, and manage one's own high expectations.

- Support her to prioritize what requires a pedal-to-the-metal approach and what can be accomplished with slower, steady progress. Discuss what is enough or more than enough at different stages and across different projects.

- Provide feedback on her impact, highlighting what is working and what needs development. Help her see that outpacing others can hurt more than it helps and is not sustainable for the team or for her over the long term.

- Call out biased feedback if team members are reacting differently to a woman than they would to a man exhibiting the same aggression and drive.

- Consider how you might be rewarding or inadvertently incenting a pedal-to-the-metal tendency. Brainstorm how you both might need to try some new practices.

Take Care to Take Charge

A pedal-to-the-metal tendency involves an incredible work ethic that knows no bounds. This may lead to overcommitting, burning the candle at both ends, and obsessing with or being too focused on work. We run on adrenaline and miss the cues that we need to slow down physically and take care of ourselves.

Adding to this success strategy is the heavy workload outside of our jobs. Research shows that when women shoulder more of the unpaid labor of caregiving and household chores, their mental health is impacted. The stress relates to the hours of work, the implicit expectations that women take on more, and the urgency around the specific chores. Same-sex couples showed less stress in regard to this issue because the discussion centered on dividing the work without the gendered assumptions of who should do what. If your pedal-to-the-metal approach occurs at home too, consider a conversation that explores what to divide or drop regardless of gender.

A 2022 Gallup–Workhuman report indicates that 25 percent of the workforce describes being burnt out "very often" or "always." Incorporating reflection, meditation, breaks from your desk, good sleep habits, and unscheduled time to think may balance you and increase your self-care, and thus give you the space and time to reconsider your fevered approach to work. I suggest journaling or using an app to track your habits and identify when enough is enough. Finding passions in areas of life outside work can also tame this tendency. Expand more of your non-work interests. Use your pedal-to-the-metal focus to hold yourself accountable to your physical and mental well-being.

KEY TAKEAWAYS

- Women who put the pedal to the metal get a ton done. We power through and drive for results as fast as we can.

- The power is in achieving results. We have high capacities and focus on the goals with an eye on the prize. We are known for working tirelessly to make things happen.

- The pitfall is that we may become so focused on and motivated by the objective that we miss bringing other perspectives or people along with us.

- At the mirrored door, we wonder why others aren't following our lead, or we sense a resistance to our attempts to rally others. We may also get stuck in place from sheer exhaustion.

- This pushing mentality becomes perilous if it leads to disconnection from our team, backlash from biased expectations, and burnout.

- The pivot is to slow down to speed up. We can create ways to build bonds, gain feedback, and take breaks to facilitate more sustainability in career and life.

JOURNAL PROMPTS

- How might you share who you are with your team for them to understand your intention, driving behavior, and areas to develop? How might you better understand them? How might you alter your usual actions to elevate others' accountability and performance?

- What did you do today to take care of yourself? What daily ritual could provide you with care and space to pause?

- Brainstorm ways that you might lighten your foot on the gas to steer your energy at a higher level; for example, block time on your calendar for ideating versus executing. What impact could you have if you focused more time and energy on strategic issues?

9

Performing Patiently

. . . .

*"If they don't give you a seat at
the table, bring a folding chair."*
SHIRLEY CHISHOLM

"**AFTER EVERYTHING** I've done, he just waltzed in and walked out with the promotion," Zoe told me, her hands curling into little balls of anger. "It's so unfair. I've always been the first one in and last one out of the office every day. I didn't argue when the previous opening went to a guy from the other office. I'm the one who restructured our whole go-to-market strategy. There wouldn't even be an open promotion if we'd not done that! I've had it."

Zoe's demeanor that day was unlike the calm, cool, and collected woman I'd first met a month ago. She'd hired me as her coach to discover how she could build her executive presence and leadership as she climbed her company's ladder. Through a few assessments, she pieced together her strengths, skills, and unique qualities. Nothing surprised her until we did an exercise that involved highlights and lowlights of one's upbringing and how they are still present for that person.

"The teachers said I was always a pleasure to have in class," she said as the smile disappeared from her face. "I was so proud when they said that at parent-teacher conferences. Years later, I remember my first boss told me, 'I wish I had ten of you. You are always on time, on budget, and so easygoing and mature. And you never give me a hard time.'"

"What does that mean to you now?" I asked.

"I always thought that was good feedback. I was the model citizen, the good worker, the one to clone. But now I feel like I'm in high school and was told I was the nicest girl in class. Yuck. Who wants to be pleasant? It's like I'm blending into the woodwork."

"How might this relate to this work issue?"

"It's like I'm following the rules, not breaking them like everyone else seems to do," Zoe said, shaking her head. "It's so frustrating because I'm so ready for this senior director role, but I haven't been good at the politics. I've been waiting my turn, and others cut the line and get rewarded. I could never do what they are doing. It feels wrong. I figured they'd take care of me when the time is right."

Performing Patiently Is Proffering

When we are successful by *performing patiently*, it means we deliver results, believe our work speaks for itself, understand our manager's timing and constraints, and are ready and eager for more when the time is right. The challenge is that the "right time" gets delayed or doesn't come.

Although the word "proffer" is not used all that often, there really is no better way to describe this success strategy of performing patiently. "To proffer" means to present for acceptance. Although it is like making an offer, proffering also involves voluntariness, spontaneity, and courtesy. As a noun, "proffer" is a suggestion. In legal circles, "proffering" refers to the point when one side makes an offer and then awaits a forthcoming response. In our careers, when we proffer, we offer up our candidacy for projects, plum assignments, and promotions, yet a follow-up offer is not guaranteed.

Like Zoe, many times women proffer their performance potential at work. On the upside, waiting patiently shows confidence in our abilities and a willingness to let our performance speak for itself. We are seen as professionals playing the long game. We signal that we are not seeking recognition for its own sake but rather for the sake of the work itself. On the downside, waiting patiently to be noticed, promoted, and/or let into the rooms where decisions are made can be risky. When we do not proactively seek opportunities for advancement or promote our own skills and achievements, we miss out on opportunities. We risk being overlooked in favor of more assertive colleagues.

When performing patiently is habitual, we ready ourselves with hope that now is finally our time, believing senior leadership knows we are waiting. We assume our excellence will be noticed and we will finally get the recognition we so richly deserve. But the workplace doesn't work that way. We must make ourselves more visible and communicate what we offer. By waiting, we are standing at the mirrored door expecting it to open so that we can be welcomed inside. When it doesn't, the unfairness, disappointment, and resentment hurt.

PERFORMING PATIENTLY: MANAGERS' CONSIDERATIONS

- Acknowledge her ability to deliver her objectives and the ease you have working with her. Appreciate that she does not overdo it with a constant focus on the next project and promotion.

- Consider how her patience makes it easy to say no or delay in favor of the person who is always asking for more. Might you need to adjust your own actions?

- Know her career goals by asking, not assuming. Tell her about the potential you see in her and co-develop a career plan for her desired future.

- Help her understand the politics of your company culture and the unwritten rules about new assignments and career advancement. Identify what is within her control and how she will be evaluated.

- Help her build her self-advocacy skills. Ask her to articulate her impact and her role in a group project so that she becomes accustomed to sharing her successes. Ask her to communicate her accomplishments with you frequently and explain that it helps you support and sponsor her.

- Collaboratively consider and build ways to increase her visibility in the organization and with senior leaders by finding opportunities for her to shine and preparing with her to be able to do so.

Conditioned to Perform Patiently

Growing up, we were rewarded for being the good girl who didn't make a fuss, cause trouble, or challenge her elders. Our behavior made it easier for those in charge, who received our obedience, compliance, and support of the unspoken rules of civility, community, and care for the greater good. Our classrooms, families, and teams needed our good behavior, and our presence mattered, as we modeled the ideal for others. It felt good to be put on a pedestal of sorts and looked at with approval.

The cues to proffer surrounded us as girls. As when we played the childhood game of "Mother May I?," we learned to ask for permission before we moved forward. As safety concerns were greater for our gender, we needed a parent's okay for many of our activities. And as we grew older, we continued to learn to play "Miss Congeniality" and unconsciously operate within a range of acceptable behaviors. While we didn't rock the boat, we likely rocked the grades, the college applications, and clubs or teams. We loved being picked, seeing our work acknowledged, and being successful. In those settings, we didn't have to do the impolite things, such as ask for what we wanted. We believed others would see our value in time. Recognition was bestowed upon us once we did the work.

The payoff has been acceptance and a positive reputation. We are easy to work with, given our understanding and patience. We engender support, assume we will be taken care of, and believe in waiting our turn for rewards. Our initial career success reinforces what we know and who we are. That's the way it works, until it doesn't.

Proactivity and presence call us to create more visibility for who we are and what we've done.

Patience Becomes Perilous

Zoe faced an organizational dynamic that felt unfamiliar. As many women find mid-career, she had shifted from being appreciated to being easy to say no to. She sought feedback and learned that she was not seen as patient but hesitant, with a lack of agency and visibility rather than the courtesy she thought she brought to the culture. She was seen as less assertive, with lower ambition than her peers, even though she quietly aspired for so much more.

Women and other marginalized people frequently fall prey to the belief that our hard work will be recognized, that others will just know what we want, and that we are ready for it. At its worst, proffering is like ringing the doorbell of the mirrored door. We are ready to be let in, gently ring the bell, but are not sure it is working. We wait to be invited in or carried over the threshold while others walk in unannounced. We are shocked by others' bravado, and then see their bold actions applauded through promotions and praise.

A recent study found a large gender gap in self-promotion, with men rating their performance 33 percent higher than equally performing women. This is particularly troubling given the pervasiveness of subjective self-assessments in many organizations that may lead others to downplay women's work. Though we may not like the idea of self-promotion, increasing our visibility is important so that we're on the radar when opportunities present themselves. The gender gap study suggested that the self-promotion gap was not related to confidence. While the evidence was not conclusive, the authors thought that women's view of self-promotion might be a factor. The study found that women did not choose to stand out, and instead were intentionally invisible and quietly getting things done, which led to them feeling liked but unfortunately undervalued. This strategy helped women avoid gendered backlash, felt more comfortable to them than a self-promoting leadership style, and provided balance for working moms, who avoided the spotlight due to their fear that exposure of their at-home responsibilities would reflect negatively on their performance.

We must find our way to open that door and get to the other side. If we don't become visible and communicate what we have done and want to do, we are giving the decision of our future to someone else who may not see us or who may have a flawed perspective. We need to pivot in the conversations we have with ourselves and our colleagues. Instead of downplaying our performance when asked for a subjective assessment, we must rely on facts to provide an objective and likely more positive picture to those around us. In place of waiting to hear of a promotion, we need to share our goals and ask how close we are and how we can get where we want to be. The risk of backlash is real, but we increase the likelihood of being overlooked if we simply lie in wait. In the spirit of playing the game to change the game, we can ascend and transcend the models of leadership to be open, proud, and humble about our performance and ambitions.

In one of our sessions, I asked Zoe, "How do you advocate for yourself?"

She searched for the right words. "I see it clearly now. I take a stand for others but sit still for myself. I've always felt that standing up for myself makes me a bad person, like it is self-centered and shameful," she said.

"How might your boss's knowledge of your ambitions and accomplishments help him?"

"He might think I'm pushy."

I asked the question again.

Zoe slowly replied, "He might finally see that I want this. That I am the best person for the team, given my work on the restructuring. He might realize that we could likely move faster with higher quality, given I know the design and have more years of experience. He'll know I mean business."

"What about your relationship with him?" I asked.

"He might start to see me in a new light. He might stop assuming I'm okay to pick up the slack and be the last one chosen. He might stop taking me, and people like me, for granted," she said, and then she declared, "I'm going to talk to him. I don't know how, but I'm going to do it. Everything I've worked for is on the line."

Many of us learned a familial or cultural judgment about standing out and/or self-promotion and the negative reaction from others. The phrase "the tallest poppy gets its head cut off" stems from a belief that there are serious risks and repercussions when we stand out above the crop. The adage is a reminder that we might be cut down to size if we poke our heads up, raise our hands for the promotion, or proactively show what we offer.

I struggled for years with self-promotion, as I associated it with too much ego and too little shame. It always seemed fake or fraudulent to me when I observed someone my mom would have described as being "too full of themselves." In our household, one of the worst things you could be was a braggart. Girls are particularly attached to these lessons and hang on to these negative beliefs into adulthood. Research shows that both men and women might fear that others won't like them if they self-promote, but women are more likely to let them stop them. They found that women have the ability to do it, but self-promotion violates their learned stereotype.

Proactivity and Presence
. . . .

If we find performing patiently an obstacle, we need to pivot to proactivity and presence. These call us to create more visibility for who we are and what we've done. That is no small task for many women. It may force us to undo self-judgment about raising our hand for a promotion. We might have to reconsider what we learned early on about proactively sharing our qualifications. When we dig deep, many discover that we have learned that asking for what we want is wrong.

Consider, though, if such well-intentioned messages hurt you in the work environment. What if they were rules of the past that no longer apply? With small steps and practice, I learned that I could share my ambitions and qualifications from a place of truth, and that helped me avoid feeling like a braggart. It felt awkward before it got comfortable, and now it feels essential. Most of all, I've received positive feedback from bosses who didn't know what I aspired to and didn't see the entirety of my work and leadership.

Zoe was nothing if not courageous. She was the daughter of immigrants who arrived in the United States with little means and big dreams. She learned to speak English through school and became the translator for her parents and extended family. This early role enabled her to bridge disparate points of view and become the collaborative team leader she is today. She settles disputes seamlessly and translates perspectives for the greater good of the project or team. She effectively moves the agendas forward but in a way that was not always seen by those above her. She had everything she needed to do the next role exceptionally well, except visibility. She had to make the case.

Zoe and I worked together to prepare her for a conversation with her manager, who previously did not see her value or potential. We used a framework I developed to help her communicate with more conviction and ease. It provided a way for her to think through what she wanted and step into this unfamiliar type of discussion. She got in touch with what mattered most to her, which shifted her from thoughts to action. The framework has four elements: stakes, intention, goals, and negotiables (aka, the SIGN framework).

Stakes. This is identifying what you have to lose and gain.

It was easy for Zoe to recognize that her career trajectory was at stake and the next level was the marker of success. When she dove deeper into why this mattered so much, she realized that she carried the hopes of her family, and that all those years of hard work from her parents led to this. This realization empowered her. She felt it was her destiny to show it was all worthwhile. This emboldened her to face the awkward, unfamiliar task of direct communication with her boss. Both her career and her family's mission were at stake.

Intention. This is your mindset and the way you want to show up in the conversation.

Once Zoe recognized her higher personal mission, she clarified her intent for this meeting with her manager. She wanted to share her accomplishments, way of leading, and hopes for her career. When we discussed how she'd like to show up, she said she wanted to be open, brave, and curious. Those three words focused her mindset to communicate with clarity, commitment, and honesty. She also set an intention to listen with curiosity as she sought to understand more.

Goals. The short-term goal is the outcome you want from the conversation. Many times, it is what you want to communicate or learn. The long-term goal is the outcome of action that is decided or advanced in the conversation.

Through our discussions, Zoe clarified her short-term goals, which were 1) to raise awareness of her qualifications and

aspirations at the company, 2) to understand her boss's perception of her candidacy, and 3) to learn more about the selection
process for the last promotion and upcoming ones. Her long-
term goals were 1) to get to the next level and be compensated
accordingly, 2) to receive more thorough feedback from her
boss and team so she could understand how she is perceived
and assess what she needed to do to close any gaps, and 3) to
gain visibility at the senior level through presentations at the
quarterly innovation meetings and annual business plans.

She decided to maximize the focus by prioritizing the near-
term goals for the first meeting and setting a second meeting
two weeks later to revisit the next step of the first meeting and
cocreate a plan for the longer term.

Negotiables. This describes the give-and-take of the agreement
you have with the company. Most people think negotiations
mean salary, bonus, and vacation time, but there are many
more negotiable elements of the relationship such as project
assignments, direct reports, committee responsibilities, development programs, initiative leadership, and promotion timing.

Zoe had a harder time when it came to negotiables because
she felt that the company and her boss held all the power. She
also struggled with a perception of being "pushy" if she asked
for more.

"What would they do if you left?" I asked.

"Well, no one else knows the pipeline process or prototype
research methodology. I lead two launch teams as well. I am not
sure what they'd do," she said.

While exiting the company wasn't necessarily Zoe's answer,
it is helpful to consider all options when we're in this type of
situation—our own and the company's. It reinforces that we
hold power in the balance and can also show us how aggressive
we can be with our requests and how we might create a win-win
outcome. While Zoe was not in a negotiation, it was helpful to

identify what her deal breakers were and what she could concede. Similarly, it is wise to consider the same for the company.

The greatest deal breaker for her would have been lack of action on a promotion timeline. She could concede the feedback because it might involve a visible process that could set a precedent for the company. As she considered the company's situation, she recognized that they could not undo the recent promotion and that they may not have an opening at the senior director level within her timeline. This assessment helped her discuss timing and the likelihood of adding a role instead of her waiting for one to open. It also made her think through whether she'd stay without the promotion a year from now. She realized that she'd want something else to signal her value and investment in her development. It led her to consider an executive MBA or other executive education courses that might broaden her skills and network. Lastly, taking a structured, strategic approach to this discussion, she planned the agenda, her messages, and her tone. After the first meeting, she told me she felt proud, not pushy. She felt encouraged and excited to continue the conversation, and so did her boss. She shifted to patiently and *proudly* performing.

KEY TAKEAWAYS

- Women who perform patiently deliver results. We believe our work speaks for itself, understand our manager's timing and constraints, and are ready when it's our time.

- The power here is that we deliver, again and again, and are counted on to do that. We are what every manager wants—a great performer who is not breathing down their neck for a promotion.

- The pitfall is that our managers may not know what we've done or what we want. Frustration sets in when we are overlooked.

- At the mirrored door, we inadvertently stall our momentum as we wait patiently for someone to invite us in, even as others gain their entrance by opening the door themselves.

- The peril is that our performance and potential become invisible to the decision makers. Our habit of proffering gives others control over our destiny. We may be perceived as less ambitious and less achievement-oriented.

- We need to pivot our mindset by reframing self-promotion as normal collaborative career planning.

JOURNAL PROMPTS

- What would your conversations sound like if you viewed self-advocacy in a positive light?

- Write a short script in which you share your accomplishments and aspirations with your boss in the same way that you would discuss other parts of your job, such as project milestone planning.

- If you gave yourself the right to ask for what you want and share why that benefits the company, how might you show up differently? What's one thing you can do to act from that mindset?

BREAK THROUGH:
TO THE GIFTS
ACROSS THE
THRESHOLD

In Part Three, we step through the mirrored door and into our growth, grit, and gravitas. When we've moved forward through fear and challenges, we learn through experience and grow stronger, more courageous, and confident, and we know we can figure it out. We relish what's on the other side and we learn to build a community that nurtures and advances us. We celebrate owning our story as a protagonist instead of being a supporting character. We answer the call to share our voice and our vision, teach those around us by modeling the way, and open the doors wide to welcome those who are creating their own paths.

10

Courage before Confidence

. . . .

*"You gain strength, courage and confidence by every
experience in which you really stop to look fear in the face...
You must do the thing you think you cannot do."*
ELEANOR ROOSEVELT

WHEN I FINALLY got pregnant for the first time, I was thrilled. I always knew I wanted to be a mom. Following the excitement of this news, I began to question how I could make it work with my career. Work had been my focus for so long that it was tough to consider how I could fit in motherhood. But I knew I loved my job at Quaker Oats; it was who I was.

We lived in a wonderful family-friendly neighborhood in Evanston, Illinois, back then and enjoyed how our street came together for block parties, Halloween, cookouts, new babies, and dog walks. Every year, neighbors, regardless of whether they were parents, gathered for the first day of school. One morning, as we eagerly awaited the school bus, I saw one little girl trembling, tears streaming down her face. Her parents tried to calm her, putting her hand in her older brother's palm. He clasped it and coaxed her onto the bus.

"You'll be fine. You'll have fun! You're a big girl now," cried her upset parents as the bus pulled away. The image of the girl's small face and hands plastered to the window haunted me. *What if I am at work when my daughter needs me? Who will soothe my child? How am I going to do all of this?* My mind raced. The words my neighbor called to her scared little girl were also exactly what I needed to hear.

Later that day, I shared my "first day of school" emotional saga with my mentoring circle, my cherished group of nine peers who met monthly to support each other and our careers. My eyes welled up as I detailed the morning event and confided my doubt in my ability to be both an executive and a mother. Fortunately, I was talked off the ledge with my friends' stories and lessons learned. When it was time for our speaker, Sue Wellington, to join us, my mood perked up. I was about to meet the Gatorade division president for the first time. During the Q&A, I asked how she handled her big job and her role as a mom. I recall that she paused as she took in my anxious voice along with my round stomach, which forced my distance from the conference room table.

I still remember her response: "I was bullish enough to think that 80 percent of me is better than 100 percent of everyone else," she responded. And it turns out that she was right, as evidenced by the staggering juggernaut she led in the Gatorade brand. Sue not only envisioned the strategy, but she was a beloved people leader who developed a talented team and created a winning culture of innovation and collaboration.

I never related to "fake it till you make it" advice, but I was blown away by her clarity and confidence that day. While I initially thought I could never be that bold, something stuck for me. I never used the term "bullish," and I didn't have the ego to say I was better than others. Still, her idea jolted me like the lightning bolt that adorned the Gatorade bottles. I wondered how her advice could apply to me and began to try it on in my mind. I had spent years with the unsaid thought that I could run circles around some of the guys who got promoted ahead of me. Maybe her perspective could be the push I needed to enter new roles and situations with the confidence that had alluded me.

Twenty-five years later, I still carry Sue's words with me as I face new opportunities with uncertainty and doubt. I help those I teach and coach evaluate their doubt through the lens of what I call "Sue's 80/100 rule." This could include a recognition of high performance, a need to set boundaries on time, or a boost to go after something big.

Courage Is the Prerequisite

I still feel grateful that Sue inspired me with the right words at that pivotal time. When I think back to her advice, I now see that her bravado was really bravery. To be sure, if you know Sue, you know she has some confidence too, but for me the enduring message was one of courage. Over time, I began to see that Sue had the guts to bet that less than 100 percent of herself at work would suffice. She knew enough about herself to risk taking that stand instead of wallowing in worry and doubt. The confidence was the outcome of her mindset and the action that followed.

Courage is the prerequisite to confidence. Our society tells us we need confidence first. It's on the agenda of every women's conference and said far too often to women in performance reviews, wrapped up in words like "presence" and "gravitas." To be sure, how we show up does matter, as do others' perceptions of our trustworthiness, competence, and warmth. But we have to start with ourselves and understand what we can tap to move ourselves toward smart risks and growth. We can't go around our obstacles. The only way out is through.

When we face something new, uncertain, or challenging, we need courage to move from fear and doubt into action. Whether we succeed or fail, we will grow from that action. We learn from our wins or by seeing what we would do next time to avoid a loss. We learn that we can win and go after something even bigger next time. We gain the knowledge that we can fall and get back up. We know we can move forward with worries and uncertainty and still figure it out. Our courage to act builds confidence. Without action, we don't gain confidence. When we reflect on ourselves negatively in front of the mirrored door, we are searching for the confidence and certainty we think we lack. Instead, we need to tap into our courage, of which we likely have a rich reservoir.

When I coach women who come to me on a quest for confidence, they are disappointed at first in my belief that it is an outcome. The implication is that they will walk out of our session without it. But when I raise the concept of courage, their eyes open wide. I see their wheels turn as they recall and share what it took for them to accomplish their long list of achievements. Dare I say that a woman in business is inherently courageous? She has entered worlds where she historically didn't belong and, sadly, is sometimes still treated as if she doesn't fit. Women who step into their own, make their choices on their own terms, and take center stage in their life have mountains of courage. It is up to us to call on that earned trait to guide ourselves and others into action, to grow and gain the confidence that results from repeatedly tackling, and surviving, our trials and tribulations. When we face and overcome challenges, we become stronger, wiser, and more formidable.

When we face and overcome challenges, we become stronger, wiser, and more formidable.

"Swagher"
. . . .

"The women are great. I just wish they had more swagger."

I was asked to prep a high-ranking partner at a financial firm for her talk to inspire MBA women interested in her field. She was eager to see if this dynamic was true of the women she'd speak to that night.

"How do they differ from the men?" I asked.

"The guys waltz in like they own the place about once a month to ask me for their next assignment, a better office location, or a raise. It's obvious they are trying to get face time with me. I am so bowled over by how easily they ask for what they want but are in no way ready for." She added, "It's like it's their birthright. I could never have done that at their age. It's hard for me to do it now, twenty-five years into my career."

"How do the women approach it?"

She laughed. "They don't approach it at all. They seem intimidated to have a direct conversation about it, yet are the ones working the longest hours. I don't want them to bug me constantly, but I worry about how they will hold their own against the guys. They are so good at their jobs; they just don't know it yet."

As with "bullish," I don't fit with the idea of "swagger." When I pose it to my female students, most feel the same, not because they lack drive or competence, but because "swagger" is simply not a style that easily fits or is familiar. I believe women do not aspire to swagger, even though some corporate leaders may expect it. Also, women who do swagger face a greater penalty in the workplace, as it seemingly trades off the warmth and "other"-orientation expected of them. "Swagger" is a no-win situation for women, especially in male-dominated and/or aggressive work cultures.

It's time we create a middle ground, a "swagher," that shows our guts and self-assuredness on our own terms. This requires an objective knowledge of our successes, talents, and unique-ness. It requires a growth mindset with which we can let go of perfection and continuously learn on the job. And it allows us to play a bigger game of our own making. It is about saying yes to the next role that we can grow into and learn instead of saying no because we don't feel ready enough. It calls on us to recognize that men ask for what they want; we need to take a page out of their notebook, but to do it in our way. If we seek to please, we don't risk difficult discussions such as asking for what we want. If we proffer, our work and future possibilities may go unseen. Although a senior leader may complain about brazen, entitled behavior, they may also believe us if we don't think we are entitled to ask for what we want. When we can identify how our success strategies work for us or against us, we have a choice to keep the status quo or stretch in new ways with courage and commitment.

An Agile Identity

When we step into new roles or companies for the first time, we bring our strengths, strategies, and skills that have always worked so well. We showcase these but may need different tactics. In his book *What Got You Here Won't Get You There*, bestselling author and top business coach Marshall Goldsmith notes that successful people can become more successful when they adapt to the changing landscape around them. Said another way, we must be aware of who we are and what we've done and assess what is needed going forward so we can adjust and grow. For example, we must see how the marketplace has evolved or what's needed as we ascend in an organization, where, in middle management, relational softer skills and smart risk-taking might be more valuable than the spreadsheet analytics we've mastered in the first few years. Our blind spot may be in the gaps we need to fill as we grow during a transition. It takes courage to objectively assess ourselves, gain feedback to uncover more, and read our surroundings to identify how to be effective yet true to ourselves.

You may recall from chapter 7 that Herminia Ibarra calls this the Authenticity Paradox. When the way that we operated and approached our role has become ingrained in our identity and a new job requires new skills or ways of being, we may feel like our authenticity and self-image are being compromised. Doubling down on past strengths can be regressive as we strive to make the new situation work. She suggests disrupting ourselves just as companies do with their businesses. On a *WorkLife with Adam Grant* podcast episode, Ibarra shared her own example of experimentation in the classroom. She tried different teaching approaches, such as moving around the classroom, which is not her usual style, to see what might engage a new generation of students, stretch her repertoire, and yet still be within her expanding comfort zone. The catch is to assess who we are and what it will take for us to succeed in a new situation. We can close any gaps with a growth mindset of experimentation, learning, and expanding our previous knowledge and skill base.

This is a good strategy, regardless of gender, but women have the added burden of trying to succeed when there may not be many or any other women to model the way. Being the one or one of the few can inadvertently incent risk avoidance and result in women playing it safe and being seen as too cautious. Ibarra suggests redefining one's career as a portfolio to which we make additions as we learn, broaden our networks, and be more experimental and playful to try on new ways of being. We are learning as we go. If we get curious and explore how others evolve, perhaps we can experiment, evolve, and expand our skills to meet the changing world we will continue to face.

KEY TAKEAWAYS

- Conventional wisdom tells women they need more confidence. But courage comes before confidence.

- We must find our own way to swagger, or "swagher." One way is to draw inspiration from other women who have found their way.

- We are accustomed to hard work and long hours. But slightly less of our time or preparation might be enough to deliver what is needed.

- Cultural conditioning heightens women's fear of failure. If our fear of failure is bigger than the fear of moving forward with unknown results, then we risk holding ourselves back.

- The best way to start is with a small act of courage. And then another, and another, and so on as we open the mirrored door.

JOURNAL PROMPTS

- Recall a time you acted with confidence. How was that preceded by courageous conversations or actions?

- List the ways you've shown courage in your career and life.

- What is one step of courage you will take this week? Next week? The following week?

11

Creating Community Takes a Village

. . . .

"Every woman's success should be an inspiration to another. We're strongest when we cheer each other on."
SERENA WILLIAMS

USED TO THINK that going it alone was a sign of strength. The reality is, we need others to help us make our way forward. The sooner we recognize this, the faster we can open ourselves up to new perspectives, learn valuable intelligence, and gain support to get further down the road.

When we face new and/or tough terrain, we need guidance. This may come in the form of a mentor who inspires, provokes, and guides our direction. This could take the form of a one-on-one, or one-to-many, relationship, like the inspiration I felt when I heard Sue Wellington. She didn't know me but spoke to her experiences, something I do now to mentor from afar. It's critical for us to be open to help, find sources that address where we most need support, and try on ideas even when they feel new.

Research tells us that women tend to be over-mentored and under-sponsored. A sponsor is someone who knows you and

183

what you can do and advocates for you when you are not in the room. These tend to be our bosses or bosses' bosses, who are the decision makers in promotions and the assessors of long-term potential. One can't simply ask someone for sponsorship, making this a tricky relationship to create. My advice is to do your best work, express your career goals and expectations, and ask for feedback to understand your perceived strengths, areas for development, and future possibilities. I tell my students, "know the book on you" and thank someone who shares it. When we know what we want and our boss knows what we want, assuming great performance and continued development, we stand a better chance of sponsorship. A sponsor must see you in action, as they put their reputation on the line when they speak up for you. Building relationships with the decision makers can help too. I also recommend proactively offsetting any possible misperceptions. One of the challenges women may face is protective bias, such as when a boss assumes someone just back from maternity leave doesn't want a promotion, work travel, or relocation. Their intent is to protect you during this transition, but they may have assumed something that isn't true. Help your bosses and sponsors by sharing what you do and don't want, or don't know yet but will figure out.

AFTER I SHARE some new detail about a night out with another couple, my husband always looks at me with surprise. "How did you know that?" he asks.

"How did you *not* know that? Didn't you guys talk?" I respond every time, incredulous.

On average, women are known to have strong relationship-building skills, but we don't always use them when it comes to networking. When we socialize, we share ourselves and go deep with others easily and enjoy it. But when it comes to the idea of networking, many women feel it is disingenuous and manipulative, and they dread it. The Stanford University Designing

Your Life course and book offer a different view: they reframe networking as being similar to asking for directions. In a world before smartphones, we would ask for directions and most people would be willing to share. An "asking for directions" mindset allows us to lower the stakes. It helps us refocus on learning about someone else's experience and how they found their way. This reorientation to wayfinding can give us more courage to make the ask. It may also make networking more enjoyable. Instead of asking for a job, we ask to learn of someone's career shift or industry experience, which in turn may yield more coffee chats or video meetups.

I recommend that women in my program analyze how they like to interact with new people or connect deeper with acquaintances. Some may dread a large networking event but love a way to meet people through smaller interactions where they are learning or doing something together. Others may recognize they need the large events and enter them with a goal to get to know just one person at first. They experiment with ways to strike up a conversation and find the types of venues that enable that interaction. Research shows that women use networks to share knowledge that informs job searches, industry understanding, and vetting of other people. We also know that it is human to have a network that looks like us. Adding people who have different experiences and backgrounds can broaden our thinking and reach. And staying connected to those we know and who know us matters. I tell my students, "Nurture your network before you need it." That may mean brief emails or LinkedIn comments, or it could mean the occasional coffee or video chat.

I highly recommend that you develop a core group of people you can go to or gather as you consider major changes and choices. Many call it a personal board of directors, people who care enough about you to be ready to advise and speak candidly about your opportunity in an objective fashion, and who can

Nurture your network before you need it.

help you figure out what you are up for, what you want, and what is the next best step on your way to the future.

When we feel defeated, exhausted, or overwhelmed, we may be tempted to give up. This is where we search for inspiration from mentors, support from our community, and grounding in what we are striving for to build our resolve and resilience. Often, we find our way back through reflection, memories, conversations, or some symbol that reminds us of who we are. Building awareness of our "check-engine light" ensures we know when enough is enough, when to get help, or when to finally provide ourselves the time we need to pause so we can stay on track. Our own personal practice and relationships with people who care about us serve to remind us of what we are all about, what is at stake, and why we matter and do what we do. We might find that power in some other figure but must also be able to find it in ourselves. When we do, we are prepared to continue the journey and slay the dragons, internal and external, along the way.

Women Hype Women

Erin Gallagher, CEO and founder of Ella, shared an image on LinkedIn of actress Jamie Lee Curtis with her arms raised, mouth wide open, cheering at the announcement of the best actress award at the 2023 Golden Globes ceremony. Without context, it would appear Curtis was really happy with her award. Contrary to how the photo might have been interpreted, she didn't win the award. Her exuberance was for Michelle Yeoh, who won for her lead role in *Everything Everywhere All at Once*. It was a beautiful example of women supporting other women. So was Gallagher's post, which included a suggested vibe for the year: "Hype. Other. Women."

We must let go of the myth that another woman's success means that we lose. To be sure, at times, we do compete head-to-head with other candidates, but this is not what we face in daily work life. In the past, bad behavior came from a perception, and often the reality, that there was only one seat for a woman to win or lose. Research has found that senior women are often hard on other women because of gender bias in the work-place. Although women having to survive in male-dominated workspaces is increasingly a thing of the past, the problem has not been completely eradicated. We have work to do to build the number of women in leadership positions. The study con-cluded that, to change this "queen bee" dynamic, we need to fix workplaces, not women. We need to call out the behavior when we see it. If we fall into that pattern ourselves, we have to get curious about where it comes from and whether it truly benefits us or the organization. How can we build the case for increasing the number of women in the organization, which may likely be the root of this issue?

The success strategy for today's times is to follow Gallagh-er's lead and hype other women. There is strength in numbers when we do this too. Though it was a fairly diverse cabinet, women in the Obama White House cabinet famously decided to amplify each other. In meetings, they would be sure to come back to a point that a woman had raised earlier but that hadn't gained traction. They credited one another's opinions when they were usurped by the men in the room. They reinforced each other's expertise to handle new initiatives.

When one woman wins, we all win. There is too much at stake to divide ourselves when we have so much progress to make. We need to model the way and align our colleagues with us, and take note as behaviors start to change for the good.

KEY TAKEAWAYS

- A woman's network matters a lot. We should do our best to surround ourselves with people and groups who nurture and advance us.

- We need to seek out mentors to teach us how others have navigated their careers. But research tells us that women are over-mentored and under-sponsored.

- The best way to get a sponsor is to do great work, share goals, ask for feedback, and be coachable to improve performance.

- To find jobs and build relationships, women leverage their networks in different ways than men. Expanding our network of women can be a source of support in various aspects of our careers.

- When we amplify the voice and value of one woman, we do it for all women.

JOURNAL PROMPTS

- List the people who advise you, formally or informally. How might you engage with them so they can nurture you and help you advance?

- Assess your network and how you might grow it. If you let go of negative associations with networking, how might you build more and better relationships?

- What can you do to amplify the women in your company, team, and life? How will you start today?

The Making of a Protagonista

"My mother told me to be a lady. And for her,
that meant be your own person, be independent."
RUTH BADER GINSBURG

A FEW WEEKS after my father's funeral, I decided I needed change. As a way to soothe my restless soul, I rearranged the furniture in my apartment, and that kept me up well past midnight. It seemed as though decluttering my condo would do the same for my mind. I flipped over a chair to move it more easily and found moving company stickers on the underside of the upholstery. Five of them, stuck one on top of the next, marked each city I had lived in and every rung on the corporate sales ladder I had climbed by twenty-nine years old. My consumer goods company's plan for me, as a customer sales leader, would add another sticker in the next twelve months. As I peeled off the pile of stickers, I saw this previous marker of success as a symbol of being stuck. I pinned it to my small kitchen bulletin board as a badge of courage for what I knew I needed to do.

I was in a pattern of moving every eighteen months to the next city and promotion. I focused on succeeding at my current role to be ready for the next one, but never really embedded myself in the town where I lived. This made it easier to move again, but the upshot was that I disproportionately focused on work. I got used to the cycle and was rewarded for it, and it fed my interest in variety. But it also meant that others decided my fate and I went along willingly, always eager to please. They could count on me to take the next move every time. My current short-term stay in Chicago was the next step in the preordained plan to become a zone manager. The thought of saying no filled me with dread as I recalled all the opportunities they'd already given me. I couldn't imagine telling my mentor that I no longer wanted the plan.

I had been in an on-again, off-again relationship for years, through many cities. I had thought I loved him, but I was not 100 percent sure that I wanted to spend the rest of my life with him. Yet at the same time, I was so frustrated that he hadn't proposed. It was as if the proposal was the goal instead of being sure the relationship was the right thing. In fairness, why would he propose when we hadn't lived in the same city in years? I treated the situation as if he held all the cards of our future. I wasn't on equal footing in the decision, and I wasn't address-ing the underlying concerns. Underneath it all, I felt that if we married, my career would be limited. So I kept taking promo-tions to new cities, unconsciously putting distance between me and what I already knew deep down: he wanted someone with fewer aspirations than I had. And I wanted someone who truly cheered my ambitions.

In hindsight, I realize how much I was waiting in many parts of my life. I waited for the big signal of his love embod-ied in an engagement ring. I waited to find out what zone and city I would get. I held myself back wherever I lived, thinking it would be better to start new extracurricular activities once I knew how everything else would unfold.

When I lost my dad to brain cancer, I was overwhelmed with sadness mixed with relief that his pain was finally over. I felt unmoored. Coming out of this unsettling blur, I recognized that something was amiss, and it wasn't just my grief. I could see myself with fresh, albeit bloodshot, eyes, and I didn't like what I saw. With "life is short" clarity, I realized that I wasn't living my life; it was living me. I wanted so much more on my own terms. I was following everyone else's agenda in my job choice, location, relationship. But it was time to take the lead in my life. The combination of this major loss, my impending thirtieth birthday, and the reflection that my situation was good, not great, prompted me to start owning my life. I could see that I wanted change, but I didn't know what, where, or how to make that happen.

In an unforeseen twist, the short-term stint in Chicago went awry when I fell in love with the city and began to prioritize what I wanted. I decided I didn't want to relocate, broke up with the guy, and saw a new career path. I learned that sometimes our greatest loss can lead to our biggest transformation. This pivot was finally of my own making and became a new beginning. I became the main character of my story, which was both exciting and scary, and I felt alive as I charted my own course.

To take ownership of our future, we must step into the role of the protagonist and lead in our own story. You may recall from English class that the protagonist is the lead character who transforms over the course of the story. In media, women have often played a secondary role as girlfriend, wife, assistant, or in service to the main character, typically a man, whose story evolves and is centered. Historically, women have seen far fewer models in popular culture of their stories being centered in society, in addition to work and life. Taking the lead in our own lives may feel unnatural or unfamiliar, which is why we need intention and effort to proactively step into a new role for ourselves.

What Is a Protagonista?

As we take center stage in our careers and lives, we must do it on our terms, not as a man would. We can learn from the English books and great scholars, but we must find our way to be our own heroine, whom I call the "protagonista."

A protagonista is not born capable and successful. She grows through trials and tribulations and learns from successes and failures. The protagonista is flawed and imperfect yet heroic in her courage to step forward anyway. She falls and experiences the consequences of her actions and continues to get back up. She battles the antagonists, inside and around her, that halt the journey and lock her out of opportunity. She finds her courage to take risks, transform, and reach for her dreams. She gives herself permission to let go of past expectations that limit her agency and voice. A protagonista learns to embrace her authentic, best yet imperfect self to inspire growth. She recognizes that she is stronger for others when she can also achieve and stand for herself.

A protagonista is a fierce protector of others. She can lead her story without seeing herself as the center of the universe. She embraces her feminine and masculine sides and finds the bravery to let go of sky-high gendered expectations yet still carry ambitions for her future and the greater good. With care for something larger than herself, she envisions a bigger future and inspires others to join her. Her "other"-focused orientation is intertwined and balanced with what she needs. So she can both take care and take charge. She doesn't leave others behind. Her courage enables her to own and value her multiple identities and others' lived experiences with openness and respect. Through her own change, she models the transformation of that which surrounds her.

A protagonista doesn't have all the answers. Her need to impress gives way to relief when she stops the pretense and receives the surprising gifts of vulnerability and imperfection as strengths, not weaknesses. Once through that obstacle, she sees she is not alone. As she learns that she doesn't need to go it alone and finally asks for help, she gives voice to herself and others. A protagonista reveals who she is, the good and the bad. This enables her to seek out support and guidance and opens her up to the mentorship she yearns for but may have previously denied.

You can be a protagonista by living these principles:

- Give yourself **permission** to take the lead and embark on the departure from the past.

- Extend your **reach** beyond your grasp and your past.

- Take **ownership** of who you are: strengths and weaknesses, the good and bad of your story.

- Build the **tenacity** to stand back up when you get knocked down.

- **Ask** for help, feedback, and advocacy to get what you need to be your best.

- Trust your **gut** to courageously face uncertainty, address your Inner Antagonist, and open the mirrored door.

- Share **opinions** that are grounded and voiced with candor, collaboration, and care.

- Possess the **no-bility** to wisely say yes to what you want and firmly say no to what you don't.

- Accept **imperfection**, which allows you to be human, celebrate progress, and act in the face of fear.

- **Surround** yourself with people, companies, and communities that see and support you and make you feel safe.

- Tell your **truth** to enable you to be who you are and say what needs to be said.

- **Amplify** women's voices at a volume and frequency that gets heard and remembered.

A protagonista unlocks the mirrored door and moves into action. This emboldens her and encourages more growth and thoughtful risks with every adventure. When she wins, she returns as the victor for all. She feels the call of her legacy and shares the elixir of her efforts, bravery, and wisdom, and opens the mirrored door for those who follow her path.

To create this shift in ourselves, we can take our cue from the "hero's journey," made famous by Joseph Campbell, who researched comparative mythology with a focus on the hero's travels through an adventure. He identified multiple stages, from the start of the journey, when the hero sets out and almost turns back, to the initiation, when he battles and overcomes crisis, to the return as the victor to the ordinary world, with many stages in between.

Campbell's story arc can inspire our playbook on this journey. When we recognize that we are the main character in our lives, we learn that we can be part of a duo or an ensemble and still prioritize our needs. Taking center stage in our lives can feel daunting, especially when we've spent years doing the opposite. According to Campbell, there are seventeen stages. I have collapsed his work into the three overarching stages for the heroine's journey: the call, the challenge, and the convening.

As we take center stage in our careers and lives, we must do it on our terms, not as a man would.

The Call

The heroine starts her journey when a new insight sparks a change from the status quo. It inspires a shift from the familiar or normal pattern that serves as a call to move into the uncertainty. It spurs an inner wonder, a new inquiry, and recurring sense that something isn't right. It is this small kernel of regret, unrest, injustice, or exhaustion that launches her forward into the unknown. For me, the call was my awareness that others were deciding my future and I was going along on autopilot, eager to please.

Sometimes, like I did at first, we ignore the call. Frequently, our inner voice is telling us something we disregard. We think, "That can't be true," or "I could never do that," or "I don't want to rock the boat." This is resistance. We stack up our fears and self-doubts, and wish for safety, convincing ourselves not to act and to avoid the risks involved. Protagonistas pause, bring awareness to their fear, and acknowledge that a situation doesn't fit or is actively wrong, something is at stake, or someone isn't what they appeared to be. Honoring emotions and inner knowing helps us overcome resistance and commit to the quest.

As we navigate our travels, we face new experiences that may elicit fear, doubt, and instincts that tell us to turn back. We find ourselves in need of guidance that may come in the form of a mentor or helper who serves to inspire, provoke, and guide our direction. We must be open for help, to find sources that fit, and to try on new ideas even when they feel outside our comfort zone. This reaffirms our journey and encourages us for the next leg of the trip.

The Challenge

The protagonista takes on new adventures that can feel both exciting and dangerous. She will inevitably face challenges and battles that may remind her of the safety and certainty she once knew. She stays the course, though, to set up her transformation. She recognizes that the past is behind her and she is in a whole new world with new rules to figure out. She faces setbacks and forges ahead. She faces trials and wins and losses. Each experience builds her skills and strengthens her for the future.

I thought I would possibly be sick in the VP's office when I told him my decision to leave sales and stay in Chicago. I didn't know him that well but somehow felt I could not disappoint him after he chose me. I summoned my courage and finally initiated the conversation that seemed to last an eternity. His shocked expression scared me, but it evaporated faster than I imagined in my months of anticipation of the discussion.

"I'm still buying stock in Ellen Connelly," he told me. "Plus, it will help sales to have you in marketing." I smiled in puzzlement over that corporate speak and with great relief that I'd finally said what I had bottled up for so long.

I didn't know then that I could say what I wanted and why, and set a boundary, and still be perceived well, with relationships intact. I spent years worrying needlessly about how I'd handle conflict when I let others down. As I began to stand up to these challenges, I became more aware of my own needs and got better at trying to get them met. It seemed to be a lifelong process for me with each new situation.

Years later, I almost gave up on my career. I logged sixty hours a week regularly, dealt with a difficult boss, juggled my household with two kids under four and my busy husband, who headed a start-up. I continued until I learned that I was grinding my teeth, a sign that I needed to reassess. This time it was my schedule and to-do list that I rearranged, dropping some of my household perfection, improving delegation, and renewing focus on what matters.

In the next year, following my doctor's advice to get a new boss, I found a new job. And when I did, I asked for a reduced schedule as I followed the path and advice of my mentor, a part-time partner at an accounting firm and parent of twins. It took a physical issue to give me the determination to recreate my job structure. That pivotal change allowed me to replenish myself by taking more time at home so that I was ready for a bigger job a few years later.

When we feel defeated, exhausted, or overwhelmed, we may be tempted to throw in the towel. This is where we search for inspiration from mentors, support from our community, and grounding in what we are striving for—to build our resolve and resilience. Often, we find our way back through reflection, memories, conversations, or some symbol that reminds us of who we are. We see the doubled-edged sword of our strengths when they work for us and against us. We must find what we are all about, how we want to show up, and how we leverage our superpowers and dim what drags us down. We seek that power in others and learn to find it in ourselves. When we do, we are prepared to continue the journey and slay the dragons, internal and external, along the way.

The Convening

The ultimate gift comes to the protagonista on the return journey. She comes home to herself stronger, wiser, and ready for what's next. Unlike the male protagonists who savor the victory, struggle to return to the ordinary world, and pass the baton, protagonistas are called to convene and convey. They come out on the other side new people, with wisdom to share.

Our courage to travel results in the confidence to conquer for the community and convey the lessons of legacy. We convene and share our hard-fought knowledge with others and inspire future journeys. There is such satisfaction helping other women on their way to what they want. I am so grateful for the opportunity to do this as a mom, as part of my job heading the Women's Leadership Program at Kellogg, and as a board director striving for more diverse and inclusive boards and management teams.

Role Models

When I was young, I loved the few and far between stories about girls or women who had courage, spoke up, or seemed to be at the center of books, television shows, or movies. Scout Finch in *To Kill a Mockingbird* inspired me to ask questions and connect to one of my values of fairness. She was listened to and had a fight in her that was intriguing. While she wasn't clearly the protagonist, she showed a curiosity about the status quo and conviction that something wasn't right. I count her as the first protagonista that I recall.

There weren't many in those days, especially on TV. When I found one, I felt seen. I thought about what I could be in the future, and the absence of women protagonists influenced my thinking about what was and wasn't available to me. Of course, this was my perspective as a middle-class white girl. Research shows us how representation, or lack thereof, sends messages to us. A UN Women report states that the global underrepresentation of women, which is rooted in patriarchal norms and traditions, has far-reaching, detrimental consequences on the personal, economic, and future well-being of girls and women, their families, and the community at large. While we have moms, aunts, friends' parents, and teachers to influence us, our view of the possibilities as young children and teens is fairly narrow. Media and culture play a large role in how we see the role of gender. While improving, we clearly have work to do to showcase women in a more positive light.

A 2019 study confirms that media plays a major role in influencing our place in society. The fifty-six highest-grossing films from twenty countries were analyzed for character gender, their time on-screen, and the portrayal of leadership. Not surprisingly, the study found that the films show a world run by men, with women rarely the story lead. The findings indicate that the stereotypes send messages to boys and girls about what they can expect and what is expected of them in their careers and lives.

Research also shows that the top one hundred highest-grossing family films achieved a milestone in 2019, with female leads hitting parity, doubling from 24 percent in 2007 to 48 percent, with time on-screen and speaking time increased as well. Of the female characters, 32.6 percent were women of color, indicating underrepresentation relative to the US population of 38 percent. Family films that featured a leading LGBTQ2S+ character reached a historic high of 5 percent in 2018, then dropped to 2 percent in 2019 in comparison to the reported LGBTQ2S+ population of 4.5 percent in the United States in 2019. Disability representation in films hit a historic high of 8 percent in 2019.

Given the power of media on kids, improving representation could reduce the unconscious biases that influence the self-images of girls and women, along with societal expectations of them. When we see other girls and women who look like us in active roles, being leaders, speaking up, and being respected for their brains, hard work, and influence, we have a better shot of seeing our own potential to do the same. Said another way, when we see it, we can be it. It's time we recognize the media messages that typecast us into certain roles or ways of being and disrupt those conditioned expectations in favor of choosing the lead role in our careers and lives.

Rewriting Your Story with You in the Lead

I declared my intention to my boss to stay in Chicago and move into branding. I registered for a year of Second City improv classes for non-actors to force my hand to stay in Chicago. All this led to a wonderful, fulfilling career, friends for life from that class, years in the same city, and a new guy, now my husband, who loved improv too, all of which has been part of my life ever since. I learned that I had to go from waiting to leading; I had to take center stage in my life and become the main character. The start for me was understanding who I was, how others saw me, how I could contribute, and what mattered to me.

"It's a journey, not a sprint," said almost every boss I ever had—for years—about a career disappointment or mistake. I used to wonder, *Then why am I so tired, like I've run so hard?* When I was younger, I wanted to get to what I perceived was the future: the final scene, the concluding chapter, and the final leg of the trip. I see now that we have been and will always be on a journey, whether we like or not, and the road goes through many curves more frequently than I once imagined.

The key difference for women is our role on those travels. Are we the driver, interpreting the directions and deciding what's next? Are we the passenger perhaps sandwiched between others in the back seat? Could we be in "the way back," as my siblings and I used to call the dreaded place where I sat in our overcrowded station wagon with crushed legs to provide others better accommodations? Maybe we are the front seat navigator with an equal hand on the directions and the music.

Wherever you currently sit, my hope is that you travel a journey of your own making with all the uncertainty around where the road will lead but with the courage to go the distance. Start where you are and run your own race, not someone else's. My wish for you is that you celebrate the wins and misses and every milestone along the way.

KEY TAKEAWAYS

- We've been conditioned to play the supporting role throughout our lives. Many aspects of our culture, like role models or media, still reinforce that role.

- When we disrupt the status quo, we can take center stage as the protagonista, or lead character, of our own story.

- A protagonista takes care and takes charge.

JOURNAL PROMPTS

- What holds you back from playing the lead role in your life? What could support you? List actions you will take to be the protagonista.

- How might pivoting from the five perils of success help you step into being a protagonista?

Conclusion
Voices Carry

"**I FEEL LIKE** I'm hitting my head against the wall here," I muttered to Leslie, my mentor, who helped me navigate the male-dominant company culture. "What happened in there?"

"You just got 'Cindy-Lou Who'd,'" she said, dryly.

"Wait, what?" I asked, from my slumped position on her office couch. Leslie was the highest-ranking woman in the organization, and I loved debriefing with her after big meetings. I had just gone down in flames in a challenging business plan discussion and needed her always insightful perspective as I reeled from my failed attempt to highlight a major flaw in next year's operating plan assumptions.

I knew the commitment that Dave, the head of product, was recommending was not feasible or based in reality. He had brought this same irritating yet influential rah-rah speech to the prior year's meeting. I let it go then, much to my regret later. Initially, his strong presence and "we can make it happen" pitch kept me from speaking my mind. I didn't want to be seen as a wet blanket or question the clear favorite, so I thought it wise to stay silent. That wisdom went out the window when I, the head of brand marketing, got saddled with unattainable objectives. When his grand plans didn't materialize, I was quietly furious.

In a year's time, I built my courage, then confidence, and was ready to call out business issues and push for a stretch goal that was still fair and within reason. Even so, that day, when he peddled the same thing for the next year's numbers, it felt like Groundhog Day. I was sure that the CEO would agree as I politely shared my concerns and asked about the assumptions. Dave brushed my queries aside and answered other softball questions from his male peers. I asked again. He resisted. I finally suggested that we figure out how to lower the target number or add back the resources needed to achieve it.

"I'm comfortable with Dave's plan. Thank you, Ellen, let's move on," the CEO interrupted. He nodded to Dave. And with those two sentences, we had signed up for a plan we knew we couldn't deliver before the calendar year even started. Avoiding conflict and showing up positively was incented far more than the guts and intellectual honesty to face the facts of the challenging market situation. This "emperor is wearing no clothes" approach to running a business and leading a team countered what I was striving to become—a leader who had the courage to say what needed to be said.

"Do you mean Cindy-Lou Who from *How the Grinch Stole Christmas*?" I asked from Leslie's couch, more confused than consoled by that reference to the holiday film classic.

"Yes. Remember how she woke up and saw the Grinch taking the gifts, the ornaments, and the tree? She knew something was wrong. What did he say to her?"

"He told her everything will be fine?" I guessed, struggling to recall. "What does that have to do with this meeting and my career-limiting move?"

"The Grinch got her a glass of water, patted her head, and basically said, 'Go back to bed, little girl, you didn't see what you saw.' Then he went up the chimney with all the stuff."

"Oh..." I said, letting the image sink in. I straightened up. "That's exactly how it felt," I said. "I was Cindy-Lou Who'd."

Because I had already had the privilege of working with so many amazing men and women who have taught, listened to, learned from, and collaborated with me, I was thrown for a loop by that meeting. But after that day, I got back up. I declared that I wasn't going to let that happen again, there or anywhere else. Of course, there is a time to let things go and a time to hold on, and, fortunately, like many women, I know how to read the room to tell the difference. Though I felt powerless in that moment, I was empowered to use my position to get more women in those rooms to change the way the game is played. I decided I would use my voice and speak my mind, even when it is hard, to make a difference and have an impact. I hope you will too.

What We'll Be Known For

When we share our aspirations and challenges, we stand a better chance of creating a new future for ourselves and the girls and women who follow. We model the way and show what can be done. When we pair the strengths of our past approaches with new ones, we may surprise those around us. We become known for our excellence, strong relationships, agility, authenticity, collaboration, drive, and performance. Those used to us doing it all, giving without getting, bending to what others expect, exhausting ourselves, and granting others all the decision-making may feel challenged. That's okay. You can't unsee what has held you in place. And you are in good company.

Every week, I get emails from women connected to me through my courses, coaching, and articles telling me how they've stepped forward and leveled up for themselves, and are standing out and up in new ways. I shared some of their stories

Courageous women opening the mirrored door inspire and show the way.

in this book and do so in my keynotes and workshops. I am so touched by the women who share how they have put something new into action in their careers and lives. I hold their stories close to my heart, along with the questions about how to handle what still seems so pervasive in the mirrored maze of work. My life's mission is to create more seats and voices at the table, and my readers are a part of that. You play an important role as you embrace and extend the message, model courage, and make a difference. Our voices carry.

Courageous women opening the mirrored door inspire and show the way. An audience member told me that she saw my TEDx talk and decided to apply for a board seat and got it. She truly was more qualified than she realized but never before thought she had that potential. Another woman shared that her thoughtful questions and suggestions led to a shift in policy and practice for parental leave and return in her organization. The company's new approach will help new dads share the burden at home and treats the caregiving need as a priority for all. They are now in discussions about the impact of hybrid work policy on parents, have started construction on an expansion of the company's mothers' room, and allow a more flexible return after childbirth, which she hoped would be in her future.

A former client bravely began to ask powerful questions about the subjective feedback she had received. Through trial and error over several courageous conversations, she finally helped her boss see that she was held to a standard that her male peers weren't. When she was promoted to a level at which she could be in the room when promotions and potential were discussed, she actively shifted the assessment to be more objective. She successfully pushed for diverse slates for promotions and added development plans to enable women and other leaders with different backgrounds to get the experiences needed to move higher in the organization. These changes are now part of the agenda and priorities of the leadership team. Our voices can make a difference for us and our work cultures. As I used to say to my daughters, now is a time to use your outside voice.

For me, breaking through the mirrored door has led me to pair my new reputation as "that professor who is full of doubt" with top ratings in the classroom, most notably for being vulnerable and creating a safe environment for others to share. I've learned to participate earlier in the boardroom with imperfect comments, disagree without being disagreeable, and be who I am, not who I think others want. I continue to push myself too hard and offset this tendency with my quiet early mornings, which give me time to write and reflect so I can be and not just do. Crossing that threshold led me to write this book and begin this amazing, scary journey.

At its core, the idea of the mirrored door is simple. We reflect inward and believe a distorted view instead of reality and the reasonable actions that will advance us. We choose the familiar behavior that worked in the past, only to come up short in comparison to rising expectations of leadership. When we summon our courage to act in small new ways, we learn we can survive and even thrive. We learn we can figure it out, be in the game, and make a difference in our conversations, our work cultures, and our careers.

Ready, Set, Go

A couple of years after I sat dejected on Leslie's couch, I was on my way to being Cindy-Lou Who'd again when, as a board member, a senior executive at the organization disregarded and sidestepped an incisive question I'd put to him.

This time I refused to go back to sleep like Cindy-Lou, and I had allies surrounding me.

I asked it again, a different way. And then again.

Others chimed in, amplifying my voice and piling onto my point. "Can we go back to Ellen's earlier question? I don't think you fully answered it," a fellow board director finally said to the executive.

As a result, the executive learned to take me, and us, seriously and we got to a better place.

My shift from supporting player to protagonista helps me slay the inner and external antagonists that will continue to join me on this journey. It also calls me to forge ahead and embrace my own story, warts and all. I know the mirrored door will continue to show up, but my self-awareness of its arrival will be my check-engine light to know that self-knowledge, courage, and action are the antidotes. I am no longer willing to be typecast. I take center stage as the leading lady of my story. You can do the same.

You have the courage and determination to make a difference. You know your tendencies, how they were reinforced, and why they may work against you as you move to higher levels in your career. It's time to break free from the expectations and limitations that may have held you back. You have the power to break through, to create change, to inspire others, and to impact the world for the better. You can be a leader, make a difference, and advocate for what you believe in. It's time to trust your instinct that you can be so much more, and take small steps of courage that bring you closer to your goals. You are already on your way. How might you raise your visibility, voice, and valor? Go and make it happen. You've got this!

Writing a book is hard work, particularly so when you reveal yourself. I was bolstered throughout the process by the idea that this book could help women raise their hands and voices. I call to you now to use what you've learned to step into the protagonista role, to take the lead in your life, for your own well-being and for the girls and women who will follow in your footsteps. Together, we can create a world where girls learn early to raise their hands, their voices, and their futures. There is strength in numbers, so let's get to work.

You are more ready than you realize. It's time to break through what has been hidden in plain sight—the mirrored door. I look forward to seeing you on the other side. Let's go.

Acknowledgments

FIRST AND FOREMOST, I'd like to thank my family. This includes my husband, Ned, the love of my life, who has always believed in me, encouraged my ambitions, added perspective and fun to every day, and partnered with me to raise our wonderful daughters, Maggie and Katie. I thank you, girls, now women, for the gift of being a mom and for showing me what it looks like to become a protagonista at a much earlier age than I did. I adore you and am so proud as I see you both come into your own and become the people you are going to be. To my five siblings, thank you for always making me feel like you have my back, for encouraging my aspirations, and for being the humble, humorous, heartfelt foundation of my life. Mom and Dad must be looking down at us, our spouses, kids, and grandchildren with sheer joy.

If you had told me seven years ago that I'd become an author, I never would have believed it. It took a village, with one thing leading to another, starting with Kate Smith, who told me about a women's leadership position that steered me away from the CMO job I was interviewing for at Kellogg. I'm thankful former dean Sally Blount prioritized the women's initiative and that Shana Carroll, Bernie Banks, and Vicki Medvec saw my potential to build it and join the faculty. Thank you to Dean Francesca Cornelli who continues to prioritize women's leadership. I'm grateful that Brenda Ellington Booth mentored me as I taught my first MBA course and suggested a storytelling workshop, and for Paul Corona, who cheered me on always and provided a boost that my fluctuating ego needed in those early days of teaching.

Thank you to Michele Weldon, Amy Guth, Katie Orenstein, and Northwestern University for naming me a Public Voices Fellow with The OpEd Project, which taught me to find and raise my voice through writing. This eventually led to Heather Hehman and the TEDxWilmette group who added me to the speaking roster and invited me into this collaborative collective that showed me the power of women's voices.

The mirrored door metaphor was born in the writing of the TEDx talk. I don't think that would have happened without Amy Port of Heroic Public Speaking, which she co-owns and leads with her husband, Michael Port. Amy listened to my dream of authorship and assigned me to AJ Harper, my speech writing coach, during my HPS core class, which I rushed to attend weeks before the TEDx event. AJ has this fabulous way of pulling your ideas out of you through her powerful questions, expertise in writing, and relentless focus on your audience. Amid multiple paragraphs of me going on and on about the issue I see, she asked me to go back and explain that thing I'd said about the mirrored door. While it was a small part of the talk, I heard that it resonated. I would soon dive deeper into her "reader first" approach when I joined her Top Three Book Workshop. There, I truly learned to write and reveled in the supportive virtual community, especially through the pandemic. When life got in the way and I stopped and started again, AJ left the porchlight on for me. I'm so thankful for her, Laura Stone, and the support and generosity of the whole Top Three community.

I am grateful for my partnership with my publisher, Page Two, and especially for my team there, led by cofounder Trena White: Kendra Ward, Caela Moffet, Peter Cocking, Fiona Lee, Meghan O'Neill, Lorraine Toor, Steph VanderMeulen, Alison Strobel, Leonni Antono, Madelaine Manson, and Colin Rier.

I am thankful for Jenny Lisk's invaluable insights and ideas.

I'm filled with gratitude for the abundance of people who coached and taught me, shared their insights, or gave me feedback that made me better as I was climbing the corporate ladder. I'm so fortunate to have moved into small business, then board governance and academia, and still found myself surrounded by so many collaborative and insightful leaders who inspire me, not to mention my talented students who learn from and teach me every day.

Lastly, I'm thankful for all the smart, successful women who told me their stories and shared their celebrations and struggles with candor and grace. You have inspired me and this book with your vulnerability and your journeys. You continue to learn how to break through the mirrored door as you take care and take charge of your careers and lives.

Notes

Chapter 1: Raise Your Hand, Raise Your Future

p. 25 *Perfectionism is increasing over time:* See Thomas Curran and Andrew P. Hill, "Perfectionism Is Increasing, and That's Not Good News," *Harvard Business Review*, January 26, 2018, hbr.org/2018/01/perfectionism-is-increasing-and-thats-not -good-news.

p. 26 *Multiple research studies indicate:* Paul L. Hewitt, Gordon L. Flett, Wendy Turnbull-Donovan, and Samuel Mikail, "The Multidimensional Perfectionism Scale: Reliability, Validity, and Psychometric Properties in Psychiatric Samples," *Psychological Assessment* 3, no. 3 (1991): 264–68, doi.org/10.1037/1040-35 90.3.3.464.

p. 26 *Their excessively high standards:* Dana Harari, Brian W. Swider, Laurens Bujold Steed, and Amy P. Breidenthal, "Is Perfect Good? A Meta-Analysis of Perfectionism in the Workplace," *Journal of Applied Psychology* 103, no. 10 (2018): 1121–44, doi.org/10.1037/apl0000324.

p. 26 *women are less likely to apply for:* Tara Sophia Mohr, "Why Women Don't Apply for Jobs Unless They're 100% Qualified," *Harvard Business Review*, August 25, 2014, hbr.org/2014/08/ why-women-dont-apply-for-jobs-unless-theyre-100-qualified.

p. 26 *Still so much of the focus:* Sheryl Sandberg, *Lean In: Women, Work, and the Will to Lead* (New York: Knopf, 2013).

p. 26 *"Our beliefs in ourselves are important:* Katherine B. Coffman, quoted in Dina Gerdeman, "How Gender Stereotypes Kill a Woman's Self-Confidence," Harvard Business School,

Working Knowledge, February 25, 2019, hbswk.hbs.edu/item/
how-gender-stereotypes-less-than-br-greater-than-kill-a
-woman-s-less-than-br-greater-than-self-confidence.

Chapter 2: Looking Back to Move Forward

p. 36   *When women take charge:* Catalyst, "The Double-Bind Dilemma
for Women in Leadership (Infographic)," August 2, 2018,
catalyst.org/wp-content/uploads/2019/01/double_bind.pdf.

p. 36   *biases of women's facial expressions:* Marianne LaFrance,
Marvin A. Hecht, and Elizabeth Levy Paluck, "The Contingent
Smile: A Meta-Analysis of Sex Differences in Smiling,"
Psychological Bulletin 129, no. 2 (2003): 305–34, doi.org/
10.1037/0033-2909.129.2.305.

p. 36   *"resting bitch face":* Jessica Bennett, "I'm Not Mad. That's
Just My RBF." *New York Times*, August 1, 2015, nytimes.com/
2015/08/02/fashion/im-not-mad-thats-just-my-resting-b
-face.html.

p. 37   *if women don't exhibit warm nonverbal communication:*
Francine M. Deutsch, Dorothy LeBaron, and Maury March
Fryer, "What Is in a Smile?" *Psychology of Women Quarterly* 11,
no. 3 (1987): 341–52, doi.org/10.1111/j.1471-6402.1987.tb00
908.x.

p. 41   *because of our tendency as youth:* Deborah Tannen, *You Just
Don't Understand! Women and Men in Conversation* (New York:
William Morrow, 2007).

p. 41   *those early relationship behaviors stay with us:* Deborah Tannen,
"The Power of Talk: Who Gets Heard and Why," *Harvard
Business Review*, September–October 1995, hbr.org/1995/09/
the-power-of-talk-who-gets-heard-and-why.

p. 45   *women represent 48 percent:* LeanIn.Org and McKinsey &
Company, *Women in the Workplace 2022*, report, wiw-report
.s3.amazonaws.com/Women_in_the_Workplace_2022.pdf.

p. 46   *women gain far fewer:* Kim Elsesser, "New LeanIn Study:
The Broken Rung Keeping Women from Management," *Forbes*,
October 15, 2019, forbes.com/sites/kimelsesser/2019/10/15/
new-leanin-study-the-broken-rung-keeping-women-from
-management.

Chapter 3: The Mirrored Maze of Work

p. 51   *refers to that gap as the "broken rung":* LeanIn.Org and McKinsey & Company, *Women in the Workplace 2022*, report, wiw-report.s3.amazonaws.com/Women_in_the_Workplace_2022.pdf.

p. 51   *Women run just 4.8 percent:* Emma Hinchliffe, "Female CEOs Run Just 4.8% of the World's Largest Businesses on the Global 500, *Fortune*, August 3, 2022, fortune.com/2022/08/03/female-ceos-global-500-thyssenkrupp-martina-merz-cvs-karen-lynch.

p. 52   *the global pay gap persists:* United Nations, "Closing Gender Pay Gaps Is More Important Than Ever," UN News, September 18, 2022, news.un.org/en/story/2022/09/1126901.

p. 52   *women earning 88 cents on men's dollar*: Carolina Aragão, "Gender Pay Gap in U.S. Hasn't Changed Much in Two Decades," Pew Research Center, March 1, 2023, pewresearch.org/fact-tank/2021/05/25/gender-pay-gap-facts.

p. 52   *Black women in the United States are paid:* LeanIn.Org, "Black Women Aren't Paid Fairly," n.d., leanin.org/data-about-the-gender-pay-gap-for-black-women#the-pay-gap.

p. 58   *gender stereotypes that limit leadership perceptions:* See Sara Martin, "The Labyrinth to Leadership," *Monitor on Psychology* 38, no. 7 (2007): 90ff., apa.org/monitor/julaug07/labyrinth; Alice Eagly and Linda L. Carli, "Women and the Labyrinth of Leadership," *Harvard Business Review*, September 2007, hbr.org/2007/09/women-and-the-labyrinth-of-leadership; and Linda L. Carli and Alice H. Eagly, "Women Face a Labyrinth: An Examination of Metaphors for Women Leaders," *Gender in Management* 31, no. 8 (2016): 514–27, doi.org/10.1108/GM-02-2015-0007.

p. 60   *second-generation bias continues:* Herminia Ibarra, Robin J. Ely, and Deborah M. Kolb, "Women Rising: The Unseen Barriers," *Harvard Business Review*, September 2013, hbr.org/2013/09/women-rising-the-unseen-barriers.

p. 61   *Researchers refer to these traits as communal:* Shankar Vedantam, Maggie Penman, Renee Klahr, Jennifer Schmidt, and Tara Boyle, "Too Sweet, or Too Shrill? The Double Bind for Women," *Hidden Brain*, podcast, NPR, October 18, 2016, npr.org/2016/10/18/498309357/too-sweet-or-too-shrill-the-double-bind-for-women.

p. 61   *Catalyst's research found that:* "Damned or Doomed: Catalyst Study on Gender Stereotyping at Work Uncovers Double-Bind Dilemmas for Women," *Women in Management Review* 22, no. 8 (2007), doi.org/10.1108/wimr.2007.05322hab.001.

p. 61   *women strategize about how to show leadership:* Wei Zheng, Ronit Kark, and Alyson Meister, "How Women Manage the Gendered Norms of Leadership," *Harvard Business Review*, November 28, 2018, hbr.org/2018/11/how-women-manage -the-gendered-norms-of-leadership.

p. 62   *"loving critics," a term that:* Tasha Eurich, "What Self-Awareness Really Is (and How to Cultivate It)," *Harvard Business Review*, January 4, 2018, hbr.org/2018/01/what-self-awareness-really -is-and-how-to-cultivate-it.

p. 63   *women receive less actionable and vaguer feedback:* See Elena Doldor, Madeleine Wyatt, and Jo Silvester, "Research: Men Get More Actionable Feedback Than Women," *Harvard Business Review*, February 10, 2021, hbr.org/2021/02/research-men-get -more-actionable-feedback-than-women; and Shelley J. Correll and Caroline Simard, "Research: Vague Feedback Is Holding Women Back," *Harvard Business Review*, April 29, 2016, hbr.org/ 2016/04/research-vague-feedback-is-holding-women-back.

p. 63   *women were given inflated performance feedback:* Lily Jampol and Vivian Zayas, "Gendered White Lies: Women Are Given Inflated Performance Feedback Compared with Men," *Personality and Social Psychology Bulletin* 47, no. 1 (2021): 57–69, doi.org/10.1177/0146167220916622.

p. 65   *Marshall Goldsmith's "feedforward" concept:* Marshall Goldsmith, "Try Feedforward Instead of Feedback," Marshall Goldsmith (blog), n.d., marshallgoldsmith.com/articles/ try-feedforward-instead-feedback/.

p. 68   *65 percent of the women reported:* Korn Ferry Institute, *Women CEOs Speak*, 2017, report, kornferry.com/content/dam/kornferry/ docs/pdfs/kf-rockefeller-women-ceos-speak.pdf.

p. 69   *connects the rise of greedy jobs to pay inequity:* See Claudia Goldin, *Career and Family: Women's Century-Long Journey toward Equity* (Princeton: Princeton University Press, 2021); and Claudia Goldin, "The Quiet Revolution That Transformed Women's Employment, Education, and Family," *American Economic Review* 96, no. 2 (2006): 1–21, doi.org/10.1257/ 000282806777212350.

Chapter 4: The Inner Antagonist

p. 82   *"There's a fake-out in the beginning:* Susan M. Cheng, "'It's Time to Raise My Hand,'" *Harvard Gazette*, December 1, 2011, news.harvard.edu/gazette/story/2011/12/its-time-to-raise -my-hand.

p. 83   *a concept first theorized and researched:* Pauline Rose Clance and Suzanne Ament Imes, "The Impostor Phenomenon in High Achieving Women: Dynamics and Therapeutic Intervention," *Psychotherapy Theory, Research & Practice* 15, no. 3 (1978), doi.org/10.1037/h0086006.

p. 83   *70 percent of high achievers have imposter syndrome:* Valerie Young, *The Secret Thoughts of Successful Women: Why Capable People Suffer from the Impostor Syndrome and How to Thrive in Spite of It* (New York: Currency, 2011).

p. 87   *we put the onus of imposter syndrome:* Ruchika Tulshyan and Jodi-Ann Burey, "Stop Telling Women They Have Imposter Syndrome," *Harvard Business Review*, February 11, 2021, hbr.org/2021/02/stop-telling-women-they-have-imposter -syndrome.

p. 87   *outlines steps organizations need to take:* Ruchika Tulshyan and Jodi-Ann Burey, "End Imposter Syndrome in Your Workplace," *Harvard Business Review*, July 14, 2021, hbr.org/2021/07/ end-imposter-syndrome-in-your-workplace.

p. 87   *these self-beliefs shape decisions:* Pedro Bordalo, Katherine Coffman, Nicola Gennaioli, and Andrei Schleifer, "Beliefs about Gender," *American Economic Review* 109, no. 3 (2019): 739–73, doi.org/10.1257/aer.20170007.

p. 88   *"Women are more likely than men:* Dina Gerdeman, "How Gender Stereotypes Kill a Woman's Self-Confidence," Harvard Business School, *Working Knowledge*, February 25, 2019, hbswk.hbs.edu/item/how-gender-stereotypes-less-than -br-greater-than-kill-a-woman-s-less-than-br-greater-than -self-confidence.

Chapter 5: Preparing to Perfection

p. 100 *"socially prescribed perfectionism":* Joachim Stoeber, "How Other-Oriented Perfectionism Differs from Self-Oriented and Socially Prescribed Perfectionism," *Journal of Psychopathology and Behavioral Assessment* 36 (2014): 329–38, doi.org/10.1007/ s10862-013-9397-7.

p. 101　*the real issue with perfectionism:* Julian H. Childs and Joachim Stoeber, "Do You Want Me to Be Perfect? Two Longitudinal Studies on Socially Prescribed Perfectionism, Stress and Burnout in the Workplace," *Work & Stress* 26, no. 4 (2012): 347–64, doi.org/10.1080/02678373.2012.737547.

p. 101　*A recent study of emerging adults:* Aleena Susan Varughese, Ajeena Achu Biju, Aleena Sarah Varghese, Jithu Shaji Varghese, and Krupa Dinah Mathews, "Procrastination, Fear of Negative Evaluation and Perceived Stress among Emerging Adults," *International Journal of Engineering Technology and Management Sciences* 5, no. 6 (2022): doi.org/10.46647/ijetms.2022.v06i05.070.

p. 104　*perfectionism is experienced uniquely:* Katherine Hampsten, "Managing the Paradoxes of Perfection in Women's Daily Lives" (PhD diss., Texas A&M University, 2012), oaktrust.library.tamu.edu/bitstream/handle/1969.1/ETD-TAMU-2012-08-11803/HAMPSTEN-DISSERTATION.pdf.

p. 107　*a call to working women to reconsider the standards:* Tiffany Dufu, *Drop the Ball: Achieving More by Doing Less* (New York: Macmillan, 2018).

p. 107　*consider creating a framework:* Alice Boyes, "How Perfectionists Can Get Out of Their Own Way," *Harvard Business Review*, April 2, 2018, hbr.org/2018/04/how-perfectionists-can-get-out-of-their-own-way.

Chapter 6: Eagerly Pleasing

p. 112　*where disengagement is high:* See both Jim Harter, "U.S Employee Engagement Slump Continues," Gallup, Workplace, April 25, 2022, gallup.com/workplace/391922/employee-engagement-slump-continues.aspx; and Evan W. Carr, Andrew Reece, Gabriella Rosen Kellerman, and Alexi Robichaux, "The Value of Belonging at Work," *Harvard Business Review*, December 16, 2019, hbr.org/2019/12/the-value-of-belonging-at-work.

p. 115　*to be seen as both communal and agentic:* Catalyst, *The Double-Bind Dilemma for Women in Leadership: Damned If You Do, Doomed If You Don't*, report, July 15, 2008, catalyst.org/wp-content/uploads/2019/01/The_Double_Bind_Dilemma_for_Women_in_Leadership_Damned_if_You_Do_Doomed_if_You_Dont.pdf.

p. 115   *People also come to expect this orientation of us:* Herminia
Ibarra, Robin J. Ely, and Deborah M. Kolb, "Women Rising:
The Unseen Barriers," *Harvard Business Review,* September
2013, hbr.org/2013/09/women-rising-the-unseen-barriers.

p. 116   *women are judged more harshly:* Madeline E. Heilman and
Julie J. Chen, "Same Behavior, Different Consequences:
Reactions to Men's and Women's Altruistic Citizenship
Behavior," *Journal of Applied Psychology* 90, no. 3 (2005):
431–41, doi.org/10.1037/0021-9010.90.3.431.

Chapter 7: Fitting the Mold

p. 129   *be perceived as the ideal worker:* Marta McClintock-Comeaux,
"Ideal Worker," in *Sociology of Work: An Encyclopedia*, ed. Vicki
Smith (Thousand Oaks, CA: SAGE Publications, Inc., 2013),
doi.org/10.4135/9781452276199.

p. 130   *a maladaptation called "I need to fit in to rise":* Deepa
Purushothaman, Lisen Stromberg, and Lisa Kaplowitz,
"5 Harmful Ways Women Feel They Must Adapt in Corporate
America," *Harvard Business Review*, October 31, 2022,
hbr.org/2022/10/5-harmful-ways-women-feel-they-must
-adapt-in-corporate-america.

p. 131   *coined the "pet to threat" phenomenon:* Kevin Donahue, Tina
Gilbert, Melinda Halpert, and Portia Robertson Migas, "The
Infuriating Journey from Pet to Threat: How Bias Undermines
Black Women at Work," *Forbes*, June 29, 2021, forbes.com/
sites/forbeseq/2021/06/29/the-infuriating-journey-from-pet
-to-threat-how-bias-undermines-black-women-at-work.

p. 133   *cultural fit has become a new form of discrimination:* Lauren A.
Rivera, "Guess Who Doesn't Fit In at Work," *New York Times*,
May 30, 2015, nytimes.com/2015/05/31/opinion/sunday/guess
-who-doesnt-fit-in-at-work.html.

p. 133   *the conditioned view of leadership:* Kelly Shue, "Women Aren't
Promoted at Work Because Managers Underestimate Their
Potential," Yale Insights, September 17, 2021, insights.som
.yale.edu/insights/women-arent-promoted-because-managers
-underestimate-their-potential.

p. 133   *women received substantially lower "potential" ratings:*
Alan Benson, Danielle Li, and Kelly Shue, "'Potential' and the
Gender Promotion Gap," research paper, June 22, 2022,

danielle-li.github.io/assets/docs/PotentialAndTheGender
PromotionGap.pdf.

p. 135   *to truly gain the benefits of diversity:* Ruchika Tulshyan,
"*Author Talks*: Don't Call It Diverse," interview by Raju Narisetti,
McKinsey & Company, *Author Talks*, February 16, 2022,
mckinsey.com/featured-insights/mckinsey-on-books/author
-talks-dont-call-it-diverse.

p. 137   *we can grow only if we put ourselves:* Herminia Ibarra, "The
Authenticity Paradox," *Harvard Business Review*, January–
February 2015, hbr.org/2015/01/the-authenticity-paradox.

p. 138   *only 10–15 percent of people are truly self-aware:* Tasha Eurich,
*Insight: The Surprising Truth about How Others See Us, How
We See Ourselves, and Why the Answers Matter More Than We
Think* (New York: Currency, 2018).

Chapter 8: Working Pedal to the Metal

p. 150   *Understanding that gendered assumptions:* Tiffany
Trzebiatowski, Courtney McCluney, and Morela Hernandez,
"Managing the Double Bind: Women Directors' Participation
Tactics in the Gendered Boardroom," *Organization Science* 34,
no. 2 (2023): 509–986, doi.org/10.1287/orsc.2022.1599.

p. 152   *when women shoulder more of the unpaid labor:* Senhu Wang
and Lambert Zixin Li, "Double Jeopardy: The Roles of Job
Autonomy and Spousal Gender Ideology in Employed Women's
Mental Health," *Applied Research in Quality Life* 18 (2023):
473–90, doi.org/10.1007/s11482-022-10090-8.

p. 152   *25 percent of the workforce:* Bryan Robinson, "Symptoms
of Job Burnout and 7 Steps to Recovery," *Forbes*, July 4, 2022,
forbes.com/sites/bryanrobinson/2022/07/04/symptoms-of
-job-burnout-and-7-steps-to-recovery; see also Workhuman and
Gallup, *Unleashing the Human Element at Work: Transforming
Workplaces through Recognition*, May 11, 2022, workhuman
.com/resources/reports-guides/unleashing-the-human-element
-at-work-transforming-workplaces-through-recognition.

Chapter 9: Performing Patiently

p. 161   *a large gender gap in self-promotion:* Christine Exley and Judd
Kessler, "Why Don't Women Self-Promote as Much as Men?"
Harvard Business Review, December 19, 2019, hbr.org/2019/12/
why-dont-women-self-promote-as-much-as-men.

p. 163   *"the tallest poppy gets its head cut off"*: Rumeet Billan, "Successful Women Pay a Price," *Forbes*, March 6, 2019, forbes.com/sites/rumeetbillan/2019/03/06/the-tallest-poppy.

p. 163   *women have the ability*: Sophia Dembling, "Are Men Better at Selling Themselves?" *gradPSYCH Magazine*, American Psychological Association, November 2011, apa.org/gradpsych/2011/11/cover-men.

Chapter 10: Courage before Confidence

p. 179   *successful people can become more successful:* Marshall Goldsmith, with Mark Reiter, *What Got You Here Won't Get You There: How Successful People Become Even More Successful!* Revised ed. (New York: Hachette, 2007).

p. 180   *the Authenticity Paradox:* Herminia Ibarra, "The Authenticity Paradox," *Harvard Business Review*, January–February 2015, hbr.org/2015/01/the-authenticity-paradox.

p. 180   *She tried different teaching approaches:* Adam Grant, "Authenticity Is a Double-Edged Sword," *WorkLife with Adam Grant*, TED podcast, April 2020, 38:15, ted.com/talks/worklife_with_adam_grant_authenticity_is_a_double_edged_sword.

Chapter 11: Creating Community Takes a Village

p. 183   *women tend to be over-mentored and under-sponsored:* See Herminia Ibarra, "Women Are Over-Mentored (But Under-Sponsored)," *HBR IdeaCast*, podcast, August 26, 2010, episode 210, 12:48, hbr.org/podcast/2010/08/women-are-over-mentored-but-un; Herminia Ibarra, "A Lack of Sponsorship Is Keeping Women from Advancing into Leadership," *Harvard Business Review*, August 19, 2019, hbr.org/2019/08/a-lack-of-sponsorship-is-keeping-women-from-advancing-into-leadership; and Center for Creative Leadership, "Women Need a Network of Champions," March 30, 2022, ccl.org/articles/leading-effectively-articles/why-women-need-a-network-of-champions.

p. 185   *reframe networking as being similar to asking for directions:* Bill Burnett and Dave Evans, *Designing Your New Work Life: How to Thrive and Change and Find Happiness—and a New Freedom—at Work* (New York: Vintage, 2021).

p. 185   *women use networks to share knowledge:* Roberta Kwok, "To Land Top Jobs, Women Need Different Types of Networks

Than Men," *Kellogg Insight*, March 1, 2019, insight.kellogg
.northwestern.edu/article/successful-networking-men-women,
based on the following research: Yang Yang, Nitesh V. Chawla,
and Brian Uzzi, "A Network's Gender Composition and
Communication Pattern Predict Women's Leadership Success,"
Proceedings of the National Academy of Sciences 116, no. 6
(2019): 2033–38, doi.org/10.1073/pnas.1721438116.

p. 185   *develop a core group of people:* Tanja Sternbauer, "Why
Women's Networks Are Crucial," Female Factor, updated
February 14, 2022, femalefactor.global/post/why-women
-s-networks-are-crucial.

p. 185   *a personal board of directors:* Susan Stelter, "Want to
Advance in Your Career? Build Your Own Board of Directors,"
Harvard Business Review, May 9, 2022, hbr.org/2022/05/want
-to-advance-in-your-career-build-your-own-board-of-directors.

p. 187   *"Hype. Other. Women.":* See Erin Gallagher's LinkedIn post,
January 11, 2023, linkedin.com/posts/erinfgallagher_women
-support-energy-activity-7019010827722653696-R_Mr.

p. 188   *senior women are often hard on other women:* Kim Elsesser,
"Queen Bees Still Exist, But It's Not the Women We Need to Fix,"
Forbes, August 31, 2020, forbes.com/sites/kimelsesser/2020/
08/31/queen-bees-still-exist-but-its-not-the-women
-we-need-to-fix.

p. 188   *women in the Obama White House cabinet:* Mattie Kahn,
"Here's How Women Staffers in the White House Made Sure
People (er, Men) Listened to Them," *Elle*, September 15, 2016,
elle.com/culture/news/a39265/women-staffers-white
-house-amplification.

Chapter 12: The Making of a Protagonista

p. 196   *hero's travels through an adventure:* Diego Ramos, "The
Hero's Journey: Joseph Campbell's Vision of the Hero's Path,"
Medium, December 21, 2011, medium.com/@RumBlues/
the-heros-journey-joseph-campbell-s-vision-of-the-hero-s
-path-707d1ca03be9.

p. 201   *Research shows us how representation:* Aneeta Rattan, Siri
Chilazi, Oriane Georgeac, and Iris Bohnet, "Tackling the
Underrepresentation of Women in Media," *Harvard Business
Review*, June 6, 2019, hbr.org/2019/06/tackling-the
-underrepresentation-of-women-in-media.

p. 201   *the global underrepresentation of women:* UN Women, "Visualizing the Data: Women's Representation in Society," February 25, 2020, unwomen.org/en/digital-library/multimedia/2020/2/infographic-visualizing-the-data-womens-representation.

p. 202   *media plays a major role in influencing:* Plan International, Girls Get Equal, and Geena Davis Institute on Gender in Media, *Rewrite Her Story: The State of the World's Girls 2019*, report, seejane.org/wp-content/uploads/2019-rewrite-her-story-plan-international-report.pdf.

p. 202   *top one hundred highest-grossing family films:* See Geena Davis Institute on Gender in Media, *See Jane 2020 Film: Historic Gender Parity in Family Films!*, report, seejane.org/wp-content/uploads/2020-film-historic-gender-parity-in-family-films-report-4.20.pdf; and Sandra Gonzalez, "Family Films Had as Many Women in Lead Roles as Men for the First Time, New Study Finds," CNN Entertainment, March 5, 2020, cnn.com/2020/03/05/entertainment/female-leads-family-films-2019/index.html.

About
the Author

ELLEN CONNELLY TAAFFE is a clinical associate professor in management and organizations at the Kellogg School of Management at Northwestern University, where she is also the founding director of the Women's Leadership Program. She teaches the popular Personal Leadership Insights course, runs the Women's Leadership Seminar series across MBA programs, and speaks and coaches within Kellogg's Executive Education programs. Ellen is a board director on three corporate boards and a strategic advisor and executive coach to company leaders.

Prior to this, Ellen spent twenty-five years building her career, eventually holding the top brand management role in divisions of PepsiCo, Royal Caribbean, and the Whirlpool Corporation. She then became president of Smith-Dahmer Associates, now Ravel Market Research, a brand and product research consultancy, before her move into academia.

Ellen received her bachelor of science from the Warrington College of Business at the University of Florida and her master of business administration from the Kellogg School of Management. She speaks extensively on women's leadership, careers, and governance. She has been featured at national conferences and in publications such as the *Harvard Business Review, Washington Post, Bloomberg News, Forbes,* and *Kellogg Insight.*

She and her husband, Ned, live in Chicago with their teenage golden retriever, and enjoy visits from their two young adult daughters.

If you want to know more about Ellen and her work, please visit her at **ellentaaffe.com** or follow her at **linkedin.com/in/ ellentaaffe.**

LOOKING TO CONTINUE THE MIRRORED DOOR JOURNEY?

Let's stay connected and let our voices carry.

Go to **ellentaaffe.com** to sign up for my newsletter and access information, including:

- Additional articles
- Reflection frameworks and other tools
- Programs and workshops
- Bulk purchase deals
- How to book speaking engagements